Smart books are the essential primers to the key issues facing business people. They are practical guides designed to give killer approaches to key business subjects, and deliver sound principles in a style that is both informative and has attitude. They are the perfect resource for time-starved business people everywhere!

The newest **Smart** titles are:

Smart **Leadership**	JONATHAN YUDELOWITZ
Smart **Marketing**	JOHN MARIOTTI
Smart **Finance**	KEN LANGDON
Smart **Strategy**	RICHARD KOCH
Smart **Business**	JAMES LEIBERT
Smart **Risk**	ANDREW HOLMES

Also available in the Smart series:

Smart Things to Know About **Brands and Branding**	JOHN MARIOTTI
Smart Things to Know About **Change**	DAVID FIRTH
Smart Things to Know About **Consultancy**	PATRICK FORSYTH
Smart Things to Know About **CRM**	DAVID HARVEY
Smart Things to Know About **Culture**	DONNA DEEPROSE
Smart Things to Know About **Customers**	ROS JAY
Smart Things to Know About **Decision Making**	KEN LANGDON
Smart Things to Know About **E-commerce**	MIKE CUNNINGHAM
Smart Things to Know About **Growth**	TONY GRUNDY
Smart Things to Know About **Innovation and Creativity**	DENNIS SHERWOOD
Smart Things to Know About **Knowledge Management**	THOMAS KOULOPOULOS
Smart Things to Know About **Lifelong Learning**	ANDREW HOLMES
Smart Things to Know About **Managing Projects**	DONNA DEEPROSE
Smart Things to Know About **Mergers & Acquisitions**	TONY GRUNDY
Smart Things to Know About **Motivation**	DONNA DEEPROSE
Smart Things to Know About **Partnerships**	JOHN MARIOTTI
Smart Things to Know About **People Management**	DAVID FIRTH
Smart Things to Know About **Scenario Planning**	TONY KIPPENBERGER
Smart Things to Know About **Six Sigma**	ANDREW BERGER
Smart Things to Know About **Managing Talent**	STEPHANIE OVERMAN
Smart Things to Know About **Teams**	ANNEMARIE CARRACIOLO
Smart Things to Know About **Technology Management**	ANDREW HOLMES
Smart Things to Know About **Your Career**	JOHN MIDDLETON

CAPSTONE

work smarter

smart
finance

KEN LANGDON
ALAN BONHAM

Copyright © 2004 by Ken Langdon and Alan Bonham

The rights of Ken Langdon and Alan Bonham to be identified as the authors of this work has been asserted in accordance with the Copyright, Designs and Patents Act 1988

First published in 2000

This edition published in 2004 by
Capstone Publishing Ltd (a Wiley Company)
The Atrium
Southern Gate
Chichester
West Sussex PO19 8SQ
England
www.wileyeurope.com

All rights reserved. Except for the quotation of short passages for the purposes of criticism and review, no part of this publication may be reproduced, stored in a retrieval system, or transmitted, in any form or by any means, electronic, mechanical, photocopying, recording or otherwise, without the prior permission of the publisher. Requests to the publisher should be addressed to the Permissions Department, John Wiley & Sons Ltd, The Atrium, Southern Gate, Chichester, West Sussex PO19 8SQ, England, or emailed to permreq@wiley.co.uk, or faxed to (+44) 1243 770571.

CIP catalogue records for this book are available from the British Library and the US Library of Congress

ISBN 1-84112-586-5

Typeset by Forewords, 109 Oxford Road, Cowley, Oxford

Printed and bound by T.J. International Ltd, Padstow, Cornwall

10 9 8 7 6 5 4 3 2 1

This book is printed on acid-free paper responsibly manufactured from sustainable forestry in which at least two trees are planted for each one used for paper production.

Substantial discounts on bulk quantities of Capstone Books are available to corporations, professional associations and other organizations. For details contact John Wiley & Sons: tel. (+44) 1243 770441, fax (+44) 1243 770517, email corporatedevelopment@wiley.co.uk

Contents

	Preface	vii
	Introduction	1
1	What Makes Shareholders Invest?	13
2	Recording Yesterday's Progress	39
3	Understanding the Past	67
4	Analysing the Past	91
5	Monitoring the Present	115
6	Planning for the Future	147
7	Never Mind the Profits, Feel the Cashflow	159
8	Getting Money into a Business	193

Glossary	209
Answers to the Smart Tests	217
Index	221

Preface

In *Smart Things to Know about Business Finance* we will look at all aspects of business from a financial angle. If you know what makes investors choose a company to invest in, you will understand a primary driver of the business corporate strategy.

From there you need to refresh on what a profit and loss account is and remind yourself why retained profits are liabilities. You then need a quick way of calculating for yourself the ratios that tell us about the financial health of a business.

Now we go internal and explain how the management accounting system should be a force for improving individual managers' performance. Then there's budgeting. Your remuneration and promotion prospects depend on your performance against budget, so make sure you understand how they work.

Finally you need a process for proving that a pet project of yours should have the finance peoples' seal of approval. You will learn how to carry out practical investment appraisal. As a parting shot we will take this one step further and look at how you attract investment money in to start the process of building the business of your dreams.

In short, the practical guide to how a smart manager's light can shine in the finance department as well as the boardroom.

Introduction

The interview panel was nearing its final question. Sally felt comfortable now after a very nervous start. She had been nervous for good reason. If this panel did not like what she said, she could wave goodbye to the hoped for promotion into second line sales management at Compusell, the major computer manufacturer she had been with for seven pretty successful years.

"One last question from you Robert?" said the Chairman giving the floor to a financial controller whom Sally did not know, but who had a reputation for regarding sales people as 'bullshit merchants'. "Yes, OK", said Robert, "Tell me Sally, what do you regard as the relationship between a company's price/earnings ratio and the return which it needs to insist on when doing investment appraisal?" Robert leant back in his chair comfortable that his point would be well made.

Sally reached back into the recesses of her mind to try and find what the question meant. She played for a bit of time. "How do you mean?" Robert came forward again to deal the coup-de-grace "Well, keeping it very simple, if a company has a PE ratio twice as high as another's, would you expect its required internal rate of return to be higher or lower?" Sally summoned up all her confidence born from the success of the rest of the interview and replied, "I know it is a fifty–fifty shot, and it's very tempting to guess, but I think I had better say that I need notice of that question."

Driving back after the panel, which despite Robert had been a hurdle successfully leapt, Sally told herself, not for the first time, that she must do something about refreshing her knowledge of business finance.

"We're in the business of making money, not cars."

General Motors Executive

Have you ever tried to argue with a finance director? They don't play fair. They have at their disposal an army of jargon calculated to wrong foot any up and coming manager. Take managers promoted into facing new challenges. They are trained for the physical task they have been assigned, but have no experience of the bunch of financial hurdles and measures that come with the job.

Much of this financial information they feel they ought to know since they probably learnt the basics at college. Or perhaps they are finding it difficult to make the bridge from the basics at college to the real world of business they find themselves in. Another thing – they would actually understand some of this financial information if it had been expressed differently, using the same language they had been taught. It all appears to be a distraction from the job they want to do rather than an assistance in getting it done.

"Money is like a sixth sense without which you cannot make a complete use of the other five."

W. Somerset Maugham, novelist

But it's a vicious circle. If you ignore the financial side of your job you will start to lose control of the physical task. If you get behind with the administration it's only going to get worse. If you do not query figures which appear to be wrong, particularly cross charges coming in from other parts of the business, you could find yourself carrying a huge load of costs dumped on you by someone who has learnt their way around the system, and has seen you coming. Even if there is no one in your organization with such evil intent, you must not rely on the internal costing systems, they are very difficult to get right and are notoriously inaccurate. The difficulty is to make the systems keep up with changes in the organization.

If this last fact surprises you, you probably need to refresh yourself on the difference between financial accounts – the ones they publish

– and management accounts, which are meant to assist everyone to run the business and meet their objectives.

The point in the end, of course, concerns decision making. You can make a decision that seems correct for the organization but is financially wrong and vice versa. If you combine your functional skills with knowledge of the financial consequences of your decisions you are on the way to being one smart manager.

Don't confuse profit with cash

And, don't forget the finance director's army of jargon. Believe it or not, you can have huge reserves on the balance sheet and no money in the bank. You can achieve a 20% return on capital employed and go bust at the same time.

Here is a simple example of a company whose profitability is unquestionable, but whose cash position does not just threaten its ability to pay dividends, but also its ability to survive.

Going bust profitably

Here is a company making a healthy profit. In fact its return on capital employed at 20% is pretty good. There is nothing untoward either about its ability to pay its interest charges out of its profits. In fact interest accounts for less than a third of its profits before interest and tax. Here are the numbers:

Long-term debt		60.0
Shareholders' funds		40.0
Capital employed		100.0
Return on capital employed		20%
Profit before interest and tax		20.0
Interest rate	10%	
Interest		6.0
Profit before tax		14.0
Tax rate	25%	
Tax		3.5
Net profit after interest and tax		10.5

> **Going bust profitably 2**
>
> Unfortunately those numbers only show one of the implications of debt ie interest. Another one is making repayments. In this case the company has to pay back £12,000 a year on the five year loan. Now look at the numbers:
>
> | | |
> |---|---|
> | Net profit after interest and tax (as before) | 10.5 |
> | Repayments | 12.0 |
> | Net cash outflow | −1.5 |
>
> So, bad luck, they are making money and running out of cash.

Who is this book for?

If you are in the situation of the manager described above, it's certainly for you. You are probably not in the finance department, unless of course you are thinking of buying enough copies of the book to give to all the managers in production and sales, which could be good for business. (It would certainly be good for our business.)

You could be in any other function, sales, marketing, production, engineering and even research and development, with responsibility for achieving results both physical and financial. And you need to be able to deal with the finance people.

The book aims to demystify the finance function and give readers the background of smart questions and information which gives them the confidence to discuss business with accountants and finance directors. Financial people can be helpful if you know how to get the best out of them, and this book shows you how.

Don't forget that people with a tendency to blind you with science often get things wrong. Always remember that people who concen-

Introduction 5

trate on only one element of running a business often lose touch with the big picture. Take, for example, venture capitalists. Now there's a smart bunch of folk looking for opportunities to invest money in companies which are the success stories of the future while they are the struggling start-ups of the present. Their people, normally pretty well paid, must understand how to help managers run a business. But watch what they do when things get difficult.

If a company which has raised venture capital to expand hits problems – normally less sales than they were expecting – the venture capital providers come in mob handed. They employ accountants to look at the situation, they use lawyers to check the contract and they put in consultants to present the company's managers with a blueprint for how to improve matters.

It is often said of consultants that they charge a lot of money for telling you things you already knew. "Consultants? They borrow your watch to tell you the time."

This army of people have two things in common: first they cost a lot of money, and second they take a huge amount of management time in answering questions and delving for analysis and information. The simple fact is that by so doing they almost always make a difficult situation even worse. And they're supposed to be the experts. It's much better to see the problems coming by understanding the jargon behind finance and solve them yourself.

And another thing. We must stop finance people using their jargon to leave us in the dark.

Suppose you are trying to get more resources out of the big blue chip company you work for because you can see a way of deploying them which will generate profit. Before you present your proposal ask the appropriate finance person: "What financial criteria do you use to decide whether a new project should go ahead or not?

If the killer response to this "We use a hurdle rate of 22%" leaves you wrong footed, then this book will help you to continue that conversation and calculate the return on your project for yourself.

In summary:

1 Do you want to know enough about finance to be able to discuss matters with finance people?

2 Is it high time you were able to make sense out of the financial pages?

3 Does your job require you to understand company reports, your own or your suppliers or customers?

4 Would it help you in your job if you understood the financial side of investment appraisal?

5 In time to come, might you need to understand how external finance is attracted into a project or business?

If the answer to any of these questions is "Yes", then buy the book and read the next bit in the comfort of your own home. Or perhaps if you read it in the office the finance people might let you claim it on expenses.

What is the structure behind the book?

Business finance, particularly if it is described as corporate finance, sounds complicated. But essentially it is:

- The attraction of money into projects

- The monitoring of the ins and outs of money during projects

- The calculation and reporting of return, or profitability

- The use of figures to understand the health of a business, and decide what to do next

These tasks have always described the role of finance no matter what the current jargon and flavours of the month are. Indeed one of the ways of dealing with financial matters is to push the problem back into one of these areas and get back to basics.

Taking the purposes of financial reporting into flowchart form, it would look like Figure 1.

In fact, it makes an easier learning task to approach these areas in a different order. If, for example, we start by examining what proprietors, institutional investors and private investors are looking for, we start with the main drivers of businesses. For this reason we will put

Plus ça change

If you want proof that nothing in the financial world really changes consider this. In one of the books in Galsworthy's Forsyte saga, a board of directors is taking questions from the floor from investors attending a biggish company's 1891 annual general meeting. Much time was taken up with questions concerning a very small charitable donation which had been made by the company to an employee who had been injured at work.

At an AGM of a large investment trust in the 1990s there was an exact replica of this with a long discussion about a small donation which, for some reason, had been traditionally made by the company.

It just goes to show that finance baffles people into only asking questions on minor topics they can definitely understand.

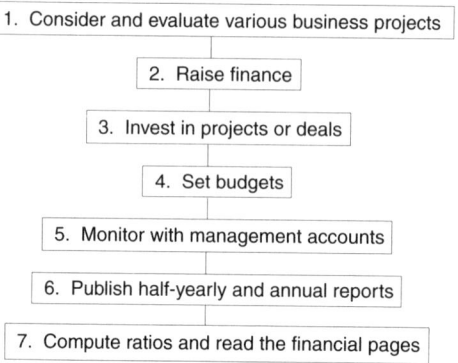

Figure 1 The corporate finance flowchart.

the reading of the financial pages into the first chapter and continue our way back up the flowchart.

The chapters then appear as follows, and readers should be able to dip into each topic more or less independently. Here, then, are the chapter headings with a one-line description of the contents.

Chapter 1: What makes shareholders invest?

Smart things to understand about the financial pages covers the topic shareholder ratios and the financial pages.

Chapter 2: Recording yesterday's progress

A smart (and fast) look at the profit and loss account, the balance sheet and the cashflow statement.

Chapter 3: Understanding the past

This chapter suggests some ratios to assess a company's strategy and financial health. It also looks at stages in a company's development.

Chapter 4: Analysing the past

> Other ratios and rules of thumb which can be found from published annual reports.

Chapter 5: Monitoring the present

> This chapter makes management accounts understandable and shows how companies monitor internal performance.

Chapter 6: Planning for the future

> Negotiating departmental objectives. This chapter deals with setting budgets in management accounts.

Chapter 7: Never mind the profits, feel the cashflow

> Assessing the costs and benefits of capital investment by using smart, and not so smart, ways of assessing the impact of projects on businesses – investment appraisal.

Chapter 8: Financing the idea

> Corporate finance – a smart look at possible sources of share and other capital.

About the authors

> It is worth mentioning how the authors came to collaborate since it is a good example of a general manager and an accountant working together and trying to make the whole greater than the sum of the parts. Ken, an experienced sales and marketing manager, was put together with Alan, an experienced accountant, by a mutual client to write and run some training events. We circled around each other for a while rather suspiciously. Ken thought that Alan might take the

realism and fun out of the training through overly strict attention to detail. Alan thought Ken might produce something which was all froth and bubble. But we got smarter and realized how a positive partnership with the finance department can lead to much better functional performance.

Of case studies, currency and checks on progress

We will illustrate how to use the information in the book by following two case study people in two very different organizations. The two people will do some financial things right but get some horribly, though understandably, wrong.

Sally Cranfield

Compusell Corporation is a major manufacturer of computer products operating in more than 100 countries world wide. They sell through two sales forces, a direct to the customer approach, and through different channels of distribution from component resellers to software houses which supply systems solutions using Compusell and other manufacturers' products.

Following her successful interview, Sally has recently become responsible for sales through distributors in the southern area of the USA. She is based in Atlanta with a boss in New York. An experienced salesperson and account manager, Sally has to get used to one major difference in the new job. The role is a profit centre. As well as looking at orders received and revenues earned, she now has to take into account the cost of sales, her and her peoples' expenses, and various assets which she will be charged with in calculating her profit performance.

She has a financial controller, based in New York, and has to learn quickly how to work with him and get him to add value to what she and her team are trying to do. This may not be easy since, as we have already seen, her knowledge of finance is rusty.

Andy McRae

Now meet Andy McRae in the UK. A Scot from Edinburgh, Andy now lives in London and has recently been dropped in at the deep end of a recruitment business HAR Ltd. It's a small business with sales revenues only a fraction of Compusell's. It was started up some seven years ago and Andy was one of its first employees. All went well until recently when a down turn in the economy caused problems first of all with sales, then with profitability and finally cash became very tight.

The shareholders blamed the Managing Director who had done well when the business was very small, but had not been able to keep up performance after a major expansion made possible by a merger.

Andy knew the business, was a key contact for a number of important customers and was given the top job on an acting basis. He is sure that he can cope with the recruitment and placement side of the business but is concerned about dealing with the investors and accountants. Like Sally it is a while since he learnt these matters and if he is not careful the new Finance Director, put in temporarily by the shareholders, will in fact run the company. Andy has to learn fast if he and the business are to survive and we will watch his progress with interest.

At a number of points in the book you will be given a chance to do a Smart Test and check it against the answers in the Appendix. These tests will help you to know if you have understood the topic in question.

Currencies

The Compusell case is in dollars and the HAR in pounds sterling. At the time of writing there are 1.6 dollars to the pound.

1 What Makes Shareholders Invest?

Introduction

One of the threads running through a smart look at business finance is the fact that all business people have in their minds a small number of ratios. They constantly monitor these performance measures to keep their job or business or part of a business on track. As we shall see this is really true of all business people from the one person building contractor to the first line manager in a megacorp, to the board of directors.

> **The independent consultant**
>
> A consultant, for example, might monitor success by calculating how many days he has billed to date compared to last year at the same time.

We are going to explore these ratios starting right at the top, with the shareholders and chairman.

Investors, the owners of a business, look to the chairman of their company to deliver his or her promises. They abhor surprises. If a chairman says "We will increase our dividends by 2% above inflation for the next three years" the City expects just that to happen and reacts very badly if it is let down. Reacting very badly means for a start that investors sell the shares. This drives down the share price. Eventually this puts more pressure on the chairman and main board directors. This pressure can become fatal to the chairman if he or she fails to reassure investors by coming up with a credible plan for putting things right. Fatal means that two or three board members might have an unstoppable urge to 'spend more time with their families' – the euphemism for leaving the company involuntarily.

Surprisingly, having been involved in the demise of these executives, the investors then allow them to go away with large sums of money to compensate them for their incompetence, but that's another story and something of a mystery.

What would be your financial and legal position if, either because you do not perform to plan or because there is a change at the top, you were fired?

So, if the chairman says that the impact she is going to have on the business will double the share value in five years, things are going to happen. Shareholders, dominated by the large insurance companies and pension funds, form a view of the board's strategy in deciding whether or not the share fits their needs. This, of course, determines the market value of the share. The directors then set strategies for profit and cashflow within the company to make sure that the company fulfils its chairman's promises.

Thus the strategy for satisfying the company's investors becomes an important driver of the company's behaviour. Another way of putting it is that the share's value reflects the market's expectation of the company's future performance.

In this first chapter we will look at how markets value a share and how shareholders decide what shares to include in their portfolios. We will do it by referring to figures which the newspapers include in

> **Smart things accountants know but don't tell you: shares**
>
> A lot of people misunderstand what capital growth of a share is. Here is a logical way of getting to that understanding. The first measure of a share's value to you is what return you can expect in the way of annual dividends. Suppose you want to buy a share which you intend to sell in three years time. Then the share is worth the sum of three year's dividends plus, of course, the value you can sell the share for at that time which you hope to be higher than the price at which you bought. This, people believe, is the capital growth.
>
> Now consider the position of the person buying the share from you. They intend to keep the share for, say, ten years. If he calculates the value of the share in the same way that you did, then his starting point is the next ten years' dividends. The capital growth that you got from him was actually his estimate of the dividend stream.
>
> Proof, if proof it be, that a share is worth the sum of future dividends over the long term not just the period that the person intends to hold the shares. If you think only in terms of the capital growth of shares it will surely catch you out.

the huge amount of data which they provide on markets, sectors and individual companies.

In later chapters we will take these ratios one level down and look at how directors and managers keep track of their performance and how analysts and journalists comment on companies.

Remember: whether you like it or not you are involved in share ownership. If there is no capital growth in the shares of the company you work for, then it runs the risk that someone will take it over and the vulnerable managers in a take-over are in the company taken over. You may have share options where capital growth is to your advantage and you may have a pension heavily invested in equities.

Learning how it works is bound to make you more aware of how to deal with these matters in your best interests.

The basics of investment

Sorry, but to make sure we are all starting at the same level let us spend a few moments looking at the basics of an investment decision. Assume you have a thousand pounds sterling which you do not have to spend now and which you are therefore going to save.

Depositing in a bank

The simplest thing you can do is to put it into a large reputable bank. This is a cheap transaction – actually it is free – and the bank will have to pay a competitive rate of interest.

Look at the interest first. What would you get at the moment for depositing £1,000? Say £60 in a full year.

This gives the yield, which is the percentage of return on the capital,

Banks

There is no capital growth in lending to a bank. They borrow money from depositors and pay them interest. They then lend the money and charge a higher rate of interest. While the interest base rate may change because of the economy, the difference between the borrowing and lending rate, the bank's profit margin, stays much the same. If there is no growth in the rate of return, there can be no capital growth. They return the same amount of money that you deposited no matter how long you leave the money with them. This leads to the smart voice – "Wonderful things banks; you give them the value of an overcoat and ten years later they return the value of a shirt."

of 6%, which is not a difficult calculation because, of course, it is the same as the rate of interest.

What else can you say about this investment? It is pretty safe. Banks do go bust but it is rare and most countries have some form of protection for depositors. It is also very liquid. That is, it is very easy to change your capital back into cash. Indeed in most cases you can do it instantaneously.

Buying shares

The situation is slightly more complicated if you decide to invest $1,000 in shares. It is usual for companies to pay their shareholders dividends once, twice or even four times a year. It's a bit like the interest you get from a bank, but is subject to the company being able to pay the dividend out of profits. Unlike interest which borrowers have to pay whatever their position, companies can 'pass', i.e. fail to pay, or reduce their dividend. This happens when the board considers that the business position requires it for the long-term future of the company.

Compusell Inc.

Right now if you invest the $1,000 in shares in Sally's company, you will get a return from dividends over a full year of about $26. This gives a gross yield of 2.6%.

So, why would anyone invest in Compusell? The answer, of course, is that there is an expectation of growth. People expect the company to grow its revenues, grow its profits and thereby be in a position to grow its dividends. This means that the share offers protection against inflation, and a better overall return in terms of dividends and capital growth.

As the dividend grows, the market tests the view of analysts and company managers to see if even more growth is possible. As long as it is, the market will revalue the shares upwards to allow for that improvement. So how do we evaluate the return? If by the end of the year the share price has increased and the value of the holding has gone up to, say, $1,050, the total return on the $1,000 investment is $76 or 7.6%, a yield of 2.6% and capital growth of 5%.

It may seem strange that we are now measuring the return by reference to the first year's dividend and the price at the end of the year, rather than by considering the value of all of the future dividends. The point is that the price at the end of the year is determined by investors in the market based on their expectations of future dividends. The price therefore already encapsulates the value of these dividends. When evaluating the performance of a share it is therefore reasonable, and straightforward, to look at the single period return as we do here for Compusell.

Other aspects of buying shares are cost and risk. We will see in a moment how much it costs to buy a share. It is obvious how much more risk there is in investing in equities rather than depositing the money in the bank. It is very easy for a market to change, for new competitors to come along and frankly for the Compusell management to make a mistake which could interrupt the growth and health of the company. In normal circumstances we expect equities to rise in value over time, but there is no guarantee of this.

To recap, the market values a company by the expectation of dividends arising in the future. This dividend stream is itself based on two assumptions. To pay a higher dividend you need higher profits and, of course, you need the cash to make the payment.

Investors are aware of the profits that the company made last year. That existing position is encapsulated in the yield. They take a view on the management and their likelihood of being successful in implementing their plans for the future. This expectation of future dividends is encapsulated in the other interesting ratio from an investors point of view which is called the *price–earnings ratio* (P/E) or the multiple. It simply records the market value of a share as a multiple of the company's earnings per share. If last year's earnings were $1 million in total and there are 1 million shares issued, then the earnings per share is $1. If the investors who are studying the likely future performance of the company are paying $20 for a share, then the price earnings ratio is 20. The P/E gives us the market's view of the future prospects of the company.

Everyone uses the historic earnings as the basis for the P/E because that is the only solid number which everybody has. If investors have taken an optimistic view of the likely growth prospects of the company the P/E will be much higher than if they regard the prospects for growth as slow.

An investment decision boils down to this: investors in a market have assessed the future prospects for a company and their view of future dividends has resulted in a market price. This market price takes into account the existing state of the company and all information available about that company.

Any new prospective investor investigates the company. Working with the same information that was available to others, prospective investors reach their own conclusions about likely future results. If they are more optimistic than the market, they may well feel the shares to be priced cheaply and may buy. Trading takes place when an individual has a different view of the future from that taken by the market as a whole. Since, of course, the market is simply the aggregate of all the individuals in that market, then the share price will adjust upwards if a number of investors all want to buy at the current market price. That is the theory and large institutional investors work that way. Many small investors do nothing like as much work as that, and put money into equities simply expecting a better performance than the bank over the long term.

HAR Plc

As an example of this, put yourself into the position of someone with enough money available to buy HAR Plc. How much would you be prepared to pay for it? There are few tangible assets in the business. It rents the accommodation it uses, does not have a stock of products and even leases the cars it gives to its employees. So there is no clue there as to how much it is worth.

We know that it has a sales revenue stream, or turnover, of £10 million. This is useful to know, but without knowing the figure for profit as well you are still not in a position to assess value. OK, here's some more information. The profits last year were £157,000, but eleven months into this year profits have dropped to even less. You now need to look at Andy, the acting managing director, very carefully. Is he going to reverse the trend and bring the profits back up, or is the continuing economic turndown going to worsen and leave HAR in a perilous situation? Difficult, huh? Well nobody said life was easy.

Look at a range of possibilities. There is still some worth in the business. It would be absurd to value it at nothing. It has been trading for seven years and has clients and candidates. It knows how to advertise for recruits, understands the industries in which it operates and works in a field which is generally growing. So it has to be worth something. Now look at the other end of the absurd spectrum. It is not worth £100 million. Even if Andy gets the profits back to £1 million, you can make better returns on £100 million than that. OK, it's up to you. Give it a value.

For the sake of this exercise we will act as a financial analyst who is in a position to talk to Andy about his business plan. We will have to make a lot of assumptions based on our analysis of the HAR plan. Assume that Andy does restore the profits during the next 18 months, and that in the long term there are attractive possibilities for merging with and taking over new firms. In five years, Andy thinks, it could be doing say five times its current business, i.e. £50 million, and if it achieves a 10% profit margin it would be making £5 million. Over the five years, therefore, the business might make £100,000, £750,000, £2,250,000, £3,750,000 and £5,000,000 – making nearly £12 million on your investment over five years. Ignoring timing and cash (which we'll come to later), the average return is £2,400,000 and you will probably have to pay at least ten times that to get the business. £24 million is a price–earnings multiple of 150 times this year's profits but only 10 times the projected average return over five years.

Before we look in the financial pages for how this is recorded, try a smart test.

> **Smart test 1**
>
> Another definition of the price–earnings ratio is that it reflects the number of years it would take the new owner to get his or her investment money back if the profits stayed the same. Is this true or false?

Stock exchange listings

The *Wall Street Journal*, the *Financial Times* (*FT*) and many other newspapers carry a complete listing of the shares traded on one or more stock exchanges. In the *FT* you will find those companies on the London Stock Exchange and the Alternative Investment Market. In the *Wall Street Journal* you will find, amongst others, the main American markets, the New York Stock Exchange and NASDAQ.

We need to take examples for the purposes of this chapter, and we will take the *Financial Times* when discussing HAR, and the *Wall Street Journal* when discussing Compusell.

The Financial Times

Towards the back of the *FT* every day, there is a complete listing of the shares which are traded on the London Stock Exchange. This is a market for second-hand shares. Buyers are people who want to start or increase a holding in a particular company and sellers are those who are holding shares which they bought earlier, either from a previous shareholder or directly from the company when the shares were initially issued.

Note that the listings are in industry sectors. This is done to ensure that readers are comparing like with like. It does not make sense to compare a telecomms company with a merchant bank. They are businesses with totally different characteristics.

Smart test 2

If something happens which makes the share price in a company plunge, as in the headline "Market chops £1 billion off the value of Badluck Plc", what impact does that have on the company's finances at that time?

Industry sectors

This sectorization is accepted in business generally. It is updated and altered regularly. HAR Plc is in the Support Services sector. Figure 1.1 gives an example of the listings page using fictitious company names.

The Support Services listings

If you go through the HAR entry item by item the first thing you see is an ace of clubs. Incidentally the legend for all of these symbols is in the bottom right-hand column of the right-hand listings page. The ace of clubs means that the company is part of the *FT* annual reports system. If you ring the telephone number mentioned or log on to their website they will send you the latest report of the company by post that day. It is a very efficient system.

	Notes	Price	+ or −	High	2004 Low	Yield	P/E	Volume '000s
Glastin	♣	249½xd	.....	255	187	1.1	28.4	–
Grinback		27	.....	37½	13½	1.9	30.5	1
HAR	♣	103½	+1	129.5	98.5	2.3	7.4	14
JY	♣	93	.....	137½	67½	3.2	7.6	21
Kingswell		338½	+26	390	280	1.6	15	5

Figure 1.1 Sample FT listing for the Support Services sector.

Back to HAR. Ignore any other small letter signs at the moment. They are explained in the legend and tend to muddy the water a bit if we go into them now.

The next item is the price, which in today's paper is 103.5 pence. But watch what happens to investors' money when they buy shares.

If we take capital of £1,000 and buy HAR shares, we will have to pay some fees. The first is to marketmakers whose profit (or turn as they call it) is represented by the spread between the price at which they will sell the share compared to the price at which they will buy. Marketmakers are the wholesalers of shares and buy and sell in large packages which they then parcel down for retail sale.

This spread is about 1–2% depending on the risk. For shares in small companies it can be even more. Competition is, however, tending to make this spread percentage lower. For the sake of example let us take 1.5% as normal and deduct £15 from our capital. It is now worth £985.

We have also to pay the stockbroker who is to the marketmaker like a retailer is to a wholesaler. Stockbrokers are very frequently part of a bank. Indeed, a lot of private investors use their banks as their stockbrokers.

Stockbrokers charge about 1.5% and also in the UK deduct the stamp duty on the transaction of 0.5%. This will cost us £15 and £5 respectively. This reduces our £1,000 to £970 and then £965.

Finally we have to remember that when we sell we will pay the stockbroker 1.5% again costing £15 and finally reducing our capital to £950. There is no need to consider the marketmakers spread here since we took the full spread between buying and selling price into account earlier.

> **Smart rule of thumb: it costs 5–6% to buy and sell shares**
>
> | | |
> |---|---|
> | Capital for investment | £1,000 |
> | Marketmakers spread at 1.5% | £15 |
> | Stockbroker's buying fee at 1.5% | £15 |
> | Stamp duty at 0.5% | £5 |
> | Stockbroker's selling fee | £15 |
> | Total costs of buying and selling | £50 or 5% of capital |
> | If the marketmakers spread were 2.5% the cost is | £60 or 6% of capital |

All this helps to remind us that, generally speaking, buying shares is a long term investment. We have to get a rise in share price of about 5% just to get back to the amount we first invested, before we start to make a profit.

Going back to the newspaper, we can now see the relevance of the price in pence. If 103.5 is the mid price, then the buying price will be about 105 and the selling price about 102. This is a spread of 3%.

Having said that, the spread is actually a good deal lower for larger companies. Large companies have frequently traded shares and there is competition amongst marketmakers. In their case, the spread could be as little as 0.5%.

xd

Beside the share price of a number of shares are the letters 'xd'. You can see one of the companies above HAR, Glastin is xd right now. This stands for ex-dividend and means that the shares are about to pay a dividend.

For 4–6 weeks before a dividend is paid the share is xd. The share register was frozen at the beginning of that period, and the dividend will be paid to the people on the register at that time. Until the dividend is paid, therefore, you buy the share xd knowing that you will not receive the next payment. Don't try to be smart about this and buy shares just before they go ex dividend on the grounds that you can make money taking the dividends and then selling the shares. First of all the market makes a minor downward adjustment to the share to allow for this, and secondly the charges for buying and selling rule it out.

Price movement

Continuing across the page, the next column shows the movement in the share during the previous day's trading. In this case HAR went up 1 pence between start and close of business yesterday, while Glastin made no movement and Kingswell went up by 26 pence, or more than 8%.

High–low

Now for the year's high and low. During the last 52 weeks HAR has been trading at a high of 129.5 and a low of 98.5: a good demonstration of the volatility of shares. Equities do go sharply up and down in value. Sometimes, as we will see, because the whole market moves sharply, and sometimes because the individual share itself has been revalued by the market because of some event in the business.

Compusell Inc.

Compusell was well known to have many contracts with the US government in Ronald Reagan's so-called Star Wars. When the announcement came that this initiative was to be severely wound down, Compusell's shares dropped dramatically.

Here is a measure of this volatility: if you had bought at the low of 98.5 and sold at the high of 129.5, you would have turned your £1,000 into £1,314 ignoring costs. In less than a year this is a very high return. If you had managed to do it the other way round, buying at 129.5 and selling at 98.5 your loss would have been 24% or your £1,000 would have become £760.

Shares do go up and down and buying and selling them is costly. Because of this they are generally recommended only for long term investment.

Yield

Back to the dividend return on investment. The yield for HAR is 2.3. This is a percentage price and reflects the dividend return you can expect if you buy the shares at today's price, 103.5, and the company pays the same amount in dividend as it did last year.

This last point is the complicating factor. Unless they have other information from published or other sources, a new investor in a company will expect the mangers to maintain or increase the annual dividend. It can only do this, of course, if it has the profits and cash

> **High and low yields**
>
> A sector which tends to have a high yield is the Electricity sector. As a utility sector it is not seen as having huge opportunities for growth. But it is a pretty safe sector since even in difficult times in the business cycle everybody still puts the lights on and cooks food.
>
> This means that people use this sector to get the relatively safe dividend income. This makes the dividend strategy generous. The share price is kept low by the perception of low growth potential in the industry. The combination of these two things gives the sector a high yield.
>
> The opposite of this is the case in, for example, Information Technology where dividends are kept relatively low to keep money in the business to fund growth and research and the share price reflects the huge opportunities which the market thinks the sector has. These two factors give the sector a low yield.

to do so. When a yield suddenly goes very high, it means that the share price has dropped significantly, and that often means that investors, i.e. the market, are unsure whether the dividend will be maintained either now or in the future.

Smart test 3

If demand forces the share price of a company up with no change to the dividend, what happens to the yield?

Price–earnings

The final number in the HAR entry is the P/E ratio. It stands at 7.4. From what you already know, this means that the total value of all the HAR shares when the price of each share is 103.5 is 7.4 times last year's earnings. (Incidentally, the words profits and earnings are interchangeable.)

But that is not the language which investors use. We have been discussing the price–earnings ratio as

P/E= market capitalization/total earnings.

Simply by dividing top and bottom of this expression by the number of shares in issue, we get the more common form of P/E ratio as

P/E= share price/earnings per share.

This last expression, earnings per share, is a very important one in the vocabulary of shareholders and their chairman as we shall see when we look at how companies present their reports in subsequent chapters.

> **Smart test 4**
>
> If a company announces an increase in its half yearly profits, but the share price stays the same, what happens to the P/E ratio?

Volume '000s

The next piece of information is the volume of shares traded yesterday. This basically comments on how seriously any price movement should be taken.

> **Smart rule of thumb**
>
> If there is a sharp movement in the day's price but a low volume changing hands, that is normally much less significant than if there has also been a major trade.

The *FT* records both the selling and buying sides of the transaction, so the number of shares involved is half of the quoted figure. Only 7,000 shares in HAR changed hands yesterday, causing a small shift in the price.

Sector averages

Having the bald numbers of the yield percentage and the P/E multiple is only useful if there is a benchmark to compare it with. The benchmark supplied on a daily basis by the *FT* is that of the average for the sector. On the back page of the companies and markets part of the *FT* there is a list of all the business sectors used in the listings page. Against each there is a lot of information calculated as an aver-

Smart rule of thumb

There are many reasons why a price–earnings ratio is very high or very low. If, for example, a company has a misleading earnings per share figure caused by an exceptional item, then it will similarly have a misleading P/E. You need to look at each case carefully. But smart rules of thumb require us to generalize and this is what different P/Es tend to mean.

If a company is in a business sector which is not expected to allow rapid growth, then the market force on the share price will keep it low in proportion to its profits and the P/E will be low. Remember, the market is looking at a company with a view to its future potential. A small company in, say, the Technology sector which could continue to grow sales by 25% or more every year for some time will be highly rated by shareholders and have a multiple of more than 50 times.

A large blue chip company in the top 100 in the UK General Retailers sector will probably not be expected to offer such growth in sales and therefore returns, and may have a P/E of 13 or 14.

During times of low inflation P/E ratios will tend to be higher than in times of high inflation. This is because the returns on cash deposits are low, forcing more money into equities. More money going into equities produces more demand than supply and prices go up. You can see the average for the whole market in the Industry sector's data.

People buying shares are, of course, interested in the chances of the company carrying out its declared strategy and producing the results anticipated by the company and business analysts. This element of risk is also built in normally to the P/E ratio. There is more chance of an ambitious plan going wrong than a limited one so generally speaking companies with a high P/E rating carry more risk than ones with a low rating.

age of a number of companies in the sector. Included among these is yield and P/E. We will use the case studies to illustrate the use of these averages.

Going back to the Support Services sector, we join Andy as he contemplates the top level of his performance measures, the share price.

HAR Plc

When Andy took over as managing director the market had rerated the whole sector and recruitment companies in particular. And they had rerated them down the way. The reason lies in the economic cycle and where people think the UK economy is in that cycle.

There had been some very good years following the recession in the early 1990s with low inflation, reduced unemployment and good growth in all sectors, particularly computers and telecommunications. This combined with the need to anticipate and neutralize the millennium bug had generated a terrific demand for permanent and temporary recruits. The recruitment companies had boomed, and HAR, with its specialization in exactly this area, had boomed more than most.

But recruitment is a leading indicator when the business cycle turns. When a fear of a slow down in business activity occurs the first thing that every company does is stop recruitment. It happens very fast. One day you can hardly field all the telephone calls, the next you are finding it tough to find enough work for all your people to do.

The average P/E reached a high of nearly 50, dropped dramatically to the high teens and had, up until Andy's tenancy at the top, recovered to 27 or 28 on rumours that maybe the feared economic hard landing might be avoided.

HAR fared worse than the sector average because the threat of recession carried more risk for their business than for others in the sector. HAR Plc was rated in the heady days at more than 70, but had gone down with a thump to the current position of 7.4.

Compusell's market rating is going in the opposite direction.

Compusell Inc.

Compusell is in the Information Technology sector, which towards the end of the 20th century was a market favourite. The opportunities for growth are still seen to be huge with "More than the population of Great Britain linking into the internet every six months."

Investors are inventing new ways of valuing companies to reflect this uncertain but hugely promising growth.

The P/E of Compusell was in the high teens for many years, but is reflecting this sector phenomenon with a P/E fluctuating between 25 and 30.

Since high P/E ratios are so common at this time, it is worth examining their real value to an investor. The shares of a company with a P/E of 25 are selling at 25 times its earnings, giving it an "earnings yield" of 4%. That is, if it pays out all its earnings in dividends, then by definition it can only yield a maximum dividend of 4% to shareholders. But companies rarely pay out all their dividends since they prefer to keep some of their earnings in the business for expansion. Generally this would reduce the yield to at most 2.5%, the rest of profits being retained.

Lending money to the government in bonds yields twice as much as that at about 5%. So if you buy shares rather than a bond you are clearly hoping for consistent above-average growth from your shares to make up the difference. So which is the better long term? In a period of low inflation it can be more difficult to justify the high valuation of a share. Suppose a share grows at twice the rate of inflation, say growth of 5% with inflation at 2.5%. It will take just short of 16 years for the dividends from shares merely to exceed the 5% yield on the bond. Even if dividend growth is four times inflation – 10% compound – it will still take eight years to get to the same income. Only if growth is an extraordinary 20% will it take less than five years for the two returns to equalize. Some companies will do this and are worth their stratospheric P/Es; many do nothing like this.

Buying a share with a high P/E may be getting on the band wagon, but buying those with a low P/E may give a better chance of beating the risk-free bond. Later on we will look at another argument which says more or less the opposite of this. Look, we told you – nobody said life was easy.

The Wall Street Journal

Before moving on to look at what the other pages in the *FT* cover, let's take time out to examine one of the US equivalents to the *FT* – the *Wall Street Journal*. The information covered is similar to the *FT* but set out differently.

Figure 1.2 is the area around the entry for Compusell. The first part

52 week High	52 week Low	Stock	Div	Yld %	PE	Vols '000	Hi	Lo	Close	Net Chg.
22¾	12¹¹⁄₁₆	CornellCorr		...		120	13	12¾	12⅞	+ ⅛
21⅛	15⁷⁄₁₆	CrnrstnPrpn	2.16	13.6	15	481	16⅛	15¾	15⅞	− ¼
118	57	Compusell	64	.8	26	28372	77½	72½	76½	+ ¾
75	34⅛	Corning	.72	1.0	38	3947	69¾	68¹⁄₁₆	68¾	− 1⅛
28¹⁵⁄₁₆	14¹⁄₁₆	CorisGp	7.70	29.9	...	889	25¹³⁄₁₆	24⅞	25¾	+ ³⁄₁₆

Figure 1.2 Sample Wall Street Journal stock market listings.

of the entry is the 52 week high and low. The name of the stock is followed by the dividend in dollars. From this and the current price we could work out the yield, but the paper does this for us in the next column. So with Compusell the high for the year is 118 and the low 57. The dividend was 64 cents per share last year giving a yield of 0.8%.

The P/E ratio follows, which at 26 is at the low end of recent fluctuations. Now comes the volume of transactions yesterday in 000s.

There is now some information that is not given in the *FT*. The next two columns show the high and low prices reached during the day – these are called the intra-day high and low. Finally we get the share price with the change which occurred during the previous day.

There are many share indices quoted in the *Wall Street Journal* of which the most famous are the Dow Jones Industrial Average and the Standards and Poor 500.

The other pages

At this stage we will just have a quick look at the other pages. The *FT* and the *Wall Street Journal* cover a lot of stories about mergers, take-

> **Smart test 5**
>
> The volume of Compusell shares is shown as 28.372 million in Figure 1.2, so how many shares changed hands yesterday?

overs and things to do with the financing and ownership of businesses. Since we will not cover that aspect of business finance until the last chapter, a brief trailer will suffice.

Notice the index at the bottom left hand of the front page of the companies section of the *FT*, an example of which is shown in Figure 1.3. The paper is well indexed and most stories are trailed in one way or another. This greatly assists the reading of the paper since it is quite simple to pick out the parts which are of relevance to you because they affect your company, your competitors, customers or

UK		Marks and Spencer	1	Deutsche Telekom	18
Albert Fisher	16	NatWest Bank	16	Elektrim18	
BAA	26	P&O	17	HFC	2
BT	17	PPM	16	Hewlett Packard	16
British Gas	17	Premier Oil	16	IBM	18
British Telecom	3	Rank	26,16	Kellogg 17	
Canary Wharf	1	Reuters 17		MediaOne	18
Co-op Bank	2	Romeike	16	MeritaNordbanken	17
Debonair	26,3	Skillsgroup	16	Olivetti	26
Emap	17	United Biscuits	16	Petronas	16
Experian	17	**Overseas**		Revlon	18
Freeserve	2	Amadeus	18	Svenska Hndlsbk	17
Glaxo Wellcome	1	Amerada Hess	16	Telecom Italia	26
GUS	17	Bank of Ireland	2	USI	18
Mansfield	16	Christiana Bank	17	Worthington Foods	17

Figure 1.3 Sample of FT contents.

suppliers. In this way you can study your industry sector quickly by use of the index.

Hold the front page

On the day of writing the *FT* has a front page story about the President Designate of the European Commission choosing his team. This is part of the economic background to commerce which any business person is well advised to keep in mind. Next to it is a piece about a Swedish car manufacturer being taken to task for using its power and influence to fix prices, by bringing its dealers together to form a type of cartel. This is a neat reminder that there is a regulatory and legal framework behind business as well as an economic one.

Vote for us, Sid

A full-page advert catches the eye. It is run by a company trying to take over the retail drinks business of a rival. The board is recommending, through this ad, that shareholders should accept its bid. "How many pints do you need to drink to think that their offer is more attractive than ours?"

We do not at this stage know whom the board of the target company wishes to succeed, assuming it wants either. The reason they might prefer one to the other will probably be a mixture of what the target company board thinks is best for their shareholders along with their personal interest in what jobs they will have in the new company. If the issue could be settled by the major shareholders, normally the big pension and unit trust funds, talking to each other this advertising approach would be unnecessary. But the board of the company placing the ad have obviously decided that the decision is close enough to require this appeal to shareholders with smaller portfolios who read the *FT*.

Even the pages which are devoted to national news in this paper have many business-oriented tinges. There is a long article about the internet and its impact on the banking sector. Next to it comes – surprise, surprise – a two-page advert from the other company mounting a bid for the drinks retailer. It gives shareholders 10 reasons why they should prefer its offer to the other one. As we will see, it is not often that small shareholders have real influence on the companies whose shares they hold, but this surely could be one of them.

The world's favourite airline.

Today's story about British Airways is a good illustration of what we get out of reading the financial pages.

- *Economic news* – One of the ways that companies economise during a period of slow growth is to limit the travel budgets of their employees. This saving comes through to BA as a reduction in the people paying premium rates to sit in business class rather than economy.

- *Currency news* – The yen has strengthened against sterling. BA is either badly prepared for this or has used the yen to hedge against other currency changes. The result is that BA has an exposure of some £790 million in yen finance which it has used to buy aircraft. This will cause a charge to the second-quarter accounts of some £69 million.

- *Industrial news* – The report says that BA had been seeking a reduction of £42 million in the wages bill for cabin crew. The staff responded to the threat to sack 1,000 people by industrial disruption, hundreds of people calling in sick, and thwarted the sackings.

- *Commodity news* – The rise in aviation fuel prices continues, with the price of a tonne going from $165 to $200. BA has hedged this by buying forward almost 70% of the fuel it needs for the second half of the year.

• *Marketing news* – BA changed the design for the tailfins on its aircraft from a simple Union flag as a signal of its country of origin. The new livery is a miscellany of abstract designs representing all the countries of the world. This was successful abroad but widely resisted at home. As a result of the bad feedback the airline has changed its mind and reprieved half of the planned tailfins. This marketing misjudgement has cost the company money and passengers.

• *Financial news* – BA's first quarter profits fell 45.6% to £94 million compared to last year. It was this announcement which triggered off the article. It is further reported that analysts are expecting the airline to do no better than break even this year compared to making a profit of £225 million last year.

• *Strategy news* – The article includes the airline's ideas for what it is going to do strategically about the situation. It intends in the future to buy smaller aircraft, which have a higher ratio of business class seats: these have a higher profit margin than economy seats. Further it intends to counter accusations of overcharging for flights in Europe by offering another cheap fares promotion. Finally it is still looking for cost savings of £225 million this year and to achieve this is going to chop 10% of its managers putting some 1,000 people off its books. This saving will cost £40 million to implement in redundancy and other charges. This gives the sub-editor the headline "BA to cut 1,000 jobs as it seeks cost savings of £225 million".

All this information was available from a ten-column-inch article; a

> **Smart test 6**
>
> In these circumstances would you call the BA shares a buy, a hold or a sell?

smart manager uses such concentrated information to keep up to date and to learn.

Analysts

The clients of stockbrokers can use what is known as an execution-only service. This is the cheapest way of using stockbrokers since they merely process the transaction you request, and have no part in advising you which shares you should buy or sell.

Alternatively you can ask the stockbroker for its advisory service and they will make recommendations for you to follow or reject. They do this, of course, for a fee. You can choose to have the stockbroker run the whole portfolio and have no part in the decision-making process at all. This tends to be the most expensive way of operating.

In the same way companies hire groups of fund managers to run the huge portfolios in the company pension scheme.

All of this creates a demand for people who become expert in particular market sectors by studying the companies and their products and markets over long periods of time. Such analysts publish their findings. To begin with they give it, for a charge, to their closest customers but eventually the information finds its way into the papers.

This information is used by journalists who are commenting on announcements from companies particularly the announcement of financial results. So an article might be written on Compusell's results like this.

Compusell Inc.: Upbeat Compusell sees shares rise

Analysts have begun upgrading profit forecasts for Compusell after the computer group delivered an upbeat earnings outlook which sent its shares soaring, and announced a link-up with internet company Servicefirst.com. This should improve its customer service particularly in small and medium size enterprises.

Compusell unveiled an 8% slide in interim pre-tax profits to $1,499 million on slightly reduced sales turnover. However, the shares put on $3 1/8 to $73 1/8 after Chief Executive Larry Godalming said that the link up will offer significant cost reductions in its Service arm.

Analysts said that the results would lead to upgrades of full year forecasts for 2003 and 2004.

We won't see those upgrades in the paper until the analysts' clients have been served.

> **Smart challenge**
>
> The main problem with reading the financial papers is the jargon they use. To become familiar with this, smart businesss people need to get into the habit of reading the financial pages regularly. What about resolving to read the Financial Times or the Wall Street Journal every Saturday for the next few months.

2 Recording Yesterday's Progress

Introduction

Good business comes from innovation, risk and customer satisfaction. But we do need some simple measures to keep control. This chapter is an introduction to the rules that govern the ways companies calculate and publish their past progress.

Businesses thrive, in the end, by selling products and services to markets. To sell products you need first to produce them. To produce them, business people need money up front. People with money are always looking for ways to invest their cash and earn a return. The joint stock company is the vehicle which brings these two things together.

Company legislation permits such companies to limit the liability of their members, shareholders, to the nominal value of their shares. In

> **Directors**
>
> The limited company enables individuals to walk away from the mess they have created under its protection, and then do it all over again somewhere else.

effect, by applying for a £1 share, a shareholder agrees to subscribe £1 and is not liable for any further contribution in the event of the company's insolvency.

Leading from the joint stock company is the need for a set of rules that directors have to obey in order to give a fair picture of the financial health of the enterprise. These are defined and developed by the accounting standards bodies of the UK and the USA. The company's auditors use these standards to monitor the company by carrying out continuous and annual audits. In theory, and often in practice, the audit is a mechanism which gives shareholders and tax authorities confidence in the values which the board use in the various financial documents they provide.

The board of directors is responsible for the stewardship of the owners' money. This stewardship involves the orderly recording of business transactions and the presentation of summary reports. This leads finally to the development of bookkeeping and accountancy.

Bookkeeping and accountancy have four main purposes:

- As a check against fraud and error

- To assist managers with the information they need to make decisions

> **Auditors**
>
> The company audit enables shareholders to sleep at night while risking bankruptcy. It is very similar to the insurance policy which permits the householder to sleep at night while their house is burgled. When they wake up to a calamity they discover, because of the small print, that they actually have no redress at all.

- As the basis for accounting practices

- To produce standards of reporting which the owners and would-be owners of a company can use to judge its past performance.

So much for the mechanisms behind public companies. In the end shareholders entrust their money to company directors who are charged with using it effectively and efficiently.

How managers use cash

Once the owners and lenders to the business have put cash into the company's bank, the company is free to start trading. It will need to spend some of the money on fixed assets – buildings, vehicles and so on – but the concentration of middle managers is on working capital. This is the cash they are using to create products and services, sell them and provide aftersales support. Their main measures come down, in the end, to how quickly the cash flows round this working capital cycle.

The general business model

To understand business finance it is useful to have a diagrammatic illustration of how money flows round a business. Figure 2.1 shows the general business model.

The capital employed in the business comes from shareholders and lenders. Share capital has the implication that the company will be expected to pay the forecast dividend. The undistributed part of a company's earnings stay in the business and belong to the shareholders. Retained profits, in most cases, increase shareholders' funds on an annual basis.

This capital goes into the company as cash, the first step in the work-

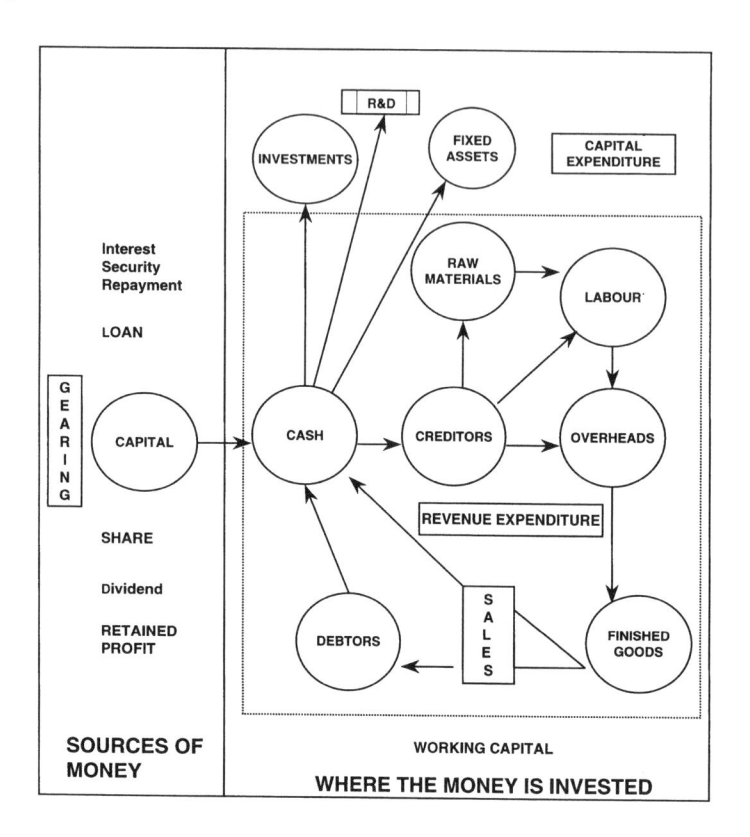

Figure 2.1 The general business model.

ing capital cycle. Managers spend this cash on, for example, raw materials, labour and overheads in the case of a manufacturer, or mainly on labour in a service business. Production thus produces a stock of finished goods which are sold to customers for either cash or credit. In a service industry there is no stock, although there may be, in slow times, idle labour. Labour is not the same as stock, of course, because you can store stock for the future; idle time is labour lost. Remember HAR in the downturn.

Also in the working capital cycle are creditors. These occur when

Supermarkets and aerospace

From the most recent accounts of a major food supermarket, Tesco, we can see that it takes less than 20 days from when they receive goods until the sales' proceeds are in their bank account. With a payment period to their creditors of about 25 days you find that all their working capital needs are funded by their creditors.

It's not so easy when you are selling complex products to customers with time to study and compare before spending large sums of money.

A leading aerospace manufacturer in the same period, BAe, holds its inventory for over 100 days before they even start to collect their money from their customers.

materials or services which this company acquires from others are supplied on credit.

Smart test 7

It obviously costs money to hold inventory (called stock in the UK). You need premises with all the associated costs of heating and lighting. You have to pay for the security of the premises, the people working in the warehouse, insurance and other things depending on the nature of the inventory.

Many companies add up these items and produce an internal figure for the cost of holding stock. They can then set targets for those costs and produce plans for reducing them.

A company has an average of £108,000 worth of inventory during a year. Managers have calculated that each day the average item in inventory costs, again on average, 0.05% of the value of the item for a day. If the average time an item stays in inventory is 40 days, what percentage of the value of stock do they have to pay out just for storing the goods they have not yet sold?

Supermarkets are an example of an industry which, because of the nature of their business, can excel in speeding cash round its working capital cycle.

So from these physical examples we can see that ideally raw materials and parts will be incorporated into the product on the day they are delivered by the supplier. In this ideal world someone will buy each product as it comes off the assembly line into stock or inventory. And finally in this commercial utopia customers will pay their bills on the day that was agreed in the contract.

In fact the world is not the ideal one described above and it takes considerable organizational effort to make businesses at least as efficient as their competitors or even with some sort of advantage to give them competitive edge.

Expenditure on items within the working capital cycle is known as

> There was a time when it was new thinking to plan to accept goods inwards "just in time". Manufacturers wanted their suppliers to deliver goods just before they were required, i.e. they were trying to create the ideal world described above. Many of their suppliers, particularly the smaller ones, found this very difficult. They found it difficult, given their chaotic business processes, to meet their customers' requirements. In fact, for some of them it was impossible to go round their order and delivery cycle inside the time their customers wanted delivery.
>
> Trying to give this service, therefore, gave rise to makeshift ways of complying. It is said that a small supplier to a Japanese motor company in the UK kept a wagonload of the parts they supplied in their customer's car park. When the call came through they instructed the driver to go from the car park to the goods inward area immediately. A good result for the car manufacturer, but an expensive solution for their supplier.

revenue expenditure, since its purpose is to create the revenue or income of the business. Revenue expense is an immediate cost which reduces the profits of the enterprise.

If a company generates profits it will normally also generate cash. Managers can use this cash for the long-term development of the business. Long-term investments are in fixed assets and research and development. A company can also invest cash in other companies buying some or all of its shares. The full cost of capital expenditure is not normally taken off the profits of the year the investment is made but spread over time. This is known as depreciation.

> **Smart rule of thumb**
>
> A person starting up a new business would be well advised to expect to need working capital of 20–30% of its forecast sales revenues.

Compusell Inc. and depreciation

Depreciation is a method of charging the cost of an asset against profits over its useful life. It is frequently misunderstood, so it is worth spending a few minutes on it now.

Suppose Compusell buys a piece of machinery for one of its factories for $65,000. The machine is expected to have scrap value of $5000 in five years' time. The $60,000 fall in value of the machine needs to be charged against profits. It would be unfair to charge the whole $60,000 in one year and so the charge is spread over the five-year useful life of the asset.

The simplest way of doing this is by charging the $60,000 equally at $12,000 per year. This is known as straight-line depreciation and is the most common method used in practice. At the end of one year the machine will be included in the balance sheet at its "net book value" of $53,000, the original cost less the charge of $12,000 for the year. At the end of the second year the net book value will be $41,000 and so on.

Notice that there is no intention that the net book value should represent the selling value of a fixed asset because there is no intention to sell the asset in the short term.

Be careful – the tax authorities insist on a different way of accounting for depreciation which we will see later.

Keep the general business model in your head as a simple template.

> **Smart things accountants may not tell us**
>
> When a company shows its valuation of fixed assets they could well be vastly out of date. They are based on historic cost, i.e. cost price minus depreciation. This figure does not necessarily give a realistic view of the assets' actual value to the business.
>
> Remember also that depreciation is a number decided on by the directors. It has no concrete meaning since, in cash terms, all the money used in buying the fixed asset may very well have already been spent.

We are going to add some complications, but none of these will invalidate this picture.

On a regular basis the finance department of the enterprise, whether internal or external, report to the shareholders on progress during the preceding period. They issue reports at the half-year stage or on a quarterly basis, but the biggest interest and publicity is given to the annual report. The next part of this chapter deals with the main financial statements, the *profit and loss account*, the *balance sheet* and the *cashflow statement*, which companies use to control their businesses and report to their owners.

The profit and loss account

Most managers are familiar with the concept of the profit and loss account. Indeed most normal people understand the concept of comparing what you are earning with what you are spending. (OK we don't necessarily count teenagers as normal people.) Let's explain the document and comment on each of the items, before showing some examples.

Terry Smith

Terry Smith is one of the smartest voices in examining the published figures of companies, particularly big blue-chip companies. In 1992 he wrote a book called Accounting for Growth (Century Business). The book achieved fame, or notoriety, by "stripping the camouflage" from the company accounts of more than 100 companies whom he named. (No wonder the jacket cover featured the words "The book they tried to ban".) Terry Smith was a catalyst in a huge number of changes to accounting standards directed at correcting the anomalies he wrote about.

It is salutary to note these, even though a lot of loopholes have since been closed. It helps to understand how smoke and mirrors were used to paint a less than frank picture of the affairs of these companies. We will also point out some places where there are still potential problems. We will put them under the heading "creative accounting". Some of these are our own, but for most of them we are indebted to Terry Smith.

The rules which correct these problems are issued as Financial Reporting Standards or FRS. We will mention which FRS corrected which anomaly so that you can read further if you wish.

Often called the earnings statement, the profit and loss account covers a period of time. In the case of most large companies they publish this statement twice a year. During the third quarter of the year they publish a profit and loss account that covers the first half of the year, including comparisons with the first half of last year. During the first quarter of the next year they publish the full year's figures.

The profit and loss account compares the sales revenue earned during a period with the costs incurred in making those sales. The figures are based on the accruals concept. That is, revenue is included for all goods dispatched whether or not payment has been received by the end of the period. Similarly, cost will include the cost

```
        Sales
        −cost of sales
    =   Gross profit
        −selling and distrubution expenses
        −administrative overheads
    =   Trading profit (earnings before interest and tax)
        −interest
    =   Net profit before tax
        −tax
    =   Profit attributable to shareholders
        −dividends
    =   Retained profit
```

Figure 2.2 The profit and loss account.

of all goods sold and services received before the end of the period. They may not have been paid for, or even invoiced, at the balance sheet date but their cost is still included.

Here is an outline of the statement together with some explanation. Remember there is always the glossary at the back of the book with more detailed definitions of financial jargon.

The top line of a profit and loss account is the sales made as you can see from Figure 2.2. These are sometimes called revenues or net revenues. Other companies use the term *sales turnover*. Be careful: "turnover" has a different meaning in the USA where it is normally reserved for "staff turnover".

From this we deduct the actual costs of the products sold. In the simple case of a bookshop it is what is paid for each of the books sold. In a manufacturing company it includes all the direct costs of producing the products sold. The jargon term usually used is *cost of sales*. A lot of managers also call these costs direct costs.

This gives us the *gross profit*. From the gross profit we can calculate the gross margin. This is a vital piece of information for monitoring purposes. How we run the business is dictated to a considerable extent by how big our gross margins are.

> **Smart tests 8 and 9**
>
> If a product costs $100 to purchase from a supplier and the sales price is $125, what is the gross margin?
>
> If a manufacturer has direct costs of manufacture of $1,000 for a product, and the sales price, governed by market forces, is $1,600, what is the gross margin?

In fact, one of the most important characteristics of a business is its gross margin, or rather gross margins since most companies sell a range of products and services which will probably have different margins. The gross margin of a product is the gross profit expressed as a percentage of the sales price.

In most cases there is a good reason for the margins that companies can achieve. For example, if there is a high level of after-sales support required, then plainly the gross margin will have to be high. The costs of after-sales service and support come out of the gross profit.

It has been interesting to watch the computer industry making the traumatic change from very high margin products like big mainframes, to tight margin equipment in the competitive world of the personal computer. So difficult was that change that almost all of them failed to make it without falling into loss. IBM lost some $9 billion by reacting too late and too slowly.

Compusell Inc.

Compusell has some good examples of high and low margins in its product range. It sells:

- Computer solutions with hardware, packaged software and tailored software solutions
- Computer systems
- Commodities and consumables such as printers and printer toner

Consider the gross margin of these product areas.

Computer solutions have a high gross margin. There is a lot of value added to the hardware by the software and consultancy which goes in to build a solution. There may be a lot of support required to ensure customer satisfaction, and that will be built into the quoted price. Remember competitors have to do the same.

At medium level are computer systems. Competitive pressures will tend to keep prices down, and in any case there is much less value added to the hardware and much of it will be a commodity mainly trading on price.

The lowest margins come in the third area where fierce competition puts heavy pressure on selling prices.

When any business person looks at the characteristics of a business, the gross margin is an important starting point.

From the gross margin we deduct the expenses. For annual reporting purposes they are divided into *selling and distribution expenses* and *administrative overheads*. It is fairly straightforward to know which is which. The costs of most of head office, for example, will go into overheads, while the costs of running the fleet of delivery vans will

Smart test 10

Which would you expect to have lower gross margins: a company selling commercial aircraft or a packaged holiday company?

be part of selling and distribution expenses. In some businesses this is a crucial distinction and some of the ratios in this area will be significant, but normally it is less important to distinguish between the two. We do not intend to pay too much attention to it. Management accounts have more detail as we will see in Chapter 5.

This gives us the *trading profit* or earnings. This is often described as earnings before interest and tax or EBIT.

Now reduce this by *interest* and you get the number for the *net profit before tax*. There is no golden rule, but this is generally the figure which people talk about when they are making comparisons. In the

Creative accounting

If a company sells a fixed asset, particularly a property, it can normally expect to make a profit. This profit is included in EBIT. Obviously it could not sell the same property again next year, so the EBIT figure is misleading. FRS 3 highlighted this by making companies show such gains separately.

There was a time when underneath this figure a company showed other expenditures under the heading Extraordinary items. The vastly important Earnings per Share figure (EPS) was at that time based on profit before these items. You can see how by always having some expenditure under this heading, which is not difficult, EPS was consistently overstated.

EPS is now based on profits after the reduction of all expenditures no matter what, so creative accountants get to work again. They show some one-off expenses under a separate column and often show an alternative EPS. Someone reading the report is thus encouraged to think that the profits are actually understated. It is interesting that very few companies show unusual or exceptional incomeseparately in the same way. But that would, of course, encourage readers to think that the profits are overstated.

business papers, when it says "the profits are down" it is probably referring to this number on the profit and loss account.

The board then spends the profits on *tax* and *dividends* before finally crediting to the shareholders the portion which they keep in the business. The *retained profit* is the item which connects the profit and loss account to the balance sheet, as we will see.

Here is the most recent profit and loss account to be published for HAR Plc:

	Notes	2003 (£000's)	2002 (£000's)
Gross fee income	1	10,284	13,856
Direct costs	2	7,676	9,645
Net fee income	3	2,608	4,211
Administrative expenses	4	1,925	1,853
Operating profit		683	2,358
Net interest payable	5	526	280
Profit on ordinary profit before taxation		157	2,078
Tax on profit on ordinary activities		24	648
Profit on ordinary activities after taxation		133	1,430
Dividends	6	225	225
Retained profit for the financial year	7	−92	1,205
Earnings per share	8	£0.14	£1.49

As Andy looks at the profit and loss account he notes the following:

1 Sales revenues dropped dramatically about halfway through the year.

2 Direct costs are the costs, salaries, expenses, etc., associated with the executives who find and make placements When there is a downturn in demand it is not possible to reduce these costs to the same extent.

3 The lower gross margin in 2002 – 25% compared to 30% the year before – is caused partly by sales difficulties producing less deals at lower selling prices and partly by the inability to reduce direct costs as indicated in (2).

4 Despite the lower sales, administrative costs are up. The company was expecting to continue its expansion, and when the trouble started these indirect costs could not be reduced quickly.

5 Interest is obviously up since we had to borrow more to bolster the cash-flow.

6 The previous MD decided to keep dividends as they were to placate the shareholders. Given the situation now, he might have been better to come clean and reduce or pass the dividend.

7 Retained profits, often called reserves, get transferred into shareholders' funds on the balance sheet.

8 The collapse in earnings per share is an inevitable result of the above problems.

The balance sheet

The balance sheet is a more difficult concept for most people to understand than the profit and loss account, but the two statements together give much better clues to the health and prospects of a company than the earnings statement on its own. Indeed at the top of a business there will be much more emphasis placed on understanding the impact of events on the balance sheet, while middle managers are more concerned with the shorter-term profit position.

One of the differences between the two documents is that a profit and loss account shows what happened over a period of time, while a balance sheet is a snapshot of the company's position at a moment in time. This moment could be any day in the financial year, but the one we are most familiar with is the balance sheet produced at the end of the company year and published with the report.

The two sides of a balance sheet, the assets and liabilities, are generally shown one on top of the other. The name of the document comes from the fact that the total of these two concepts must equal each other. Every penny that the company has, the liabilities, has to be accounted for by showing which asset it has funded or bought. Let's take it step by step. Figures 2.3 and 2.4 show the most common layouts for a US and a UK balance sheet respectively. Just to complicate matters some companies show the two sides beside each other rather than one on top of the other.

It may be difficult to believe but the different terms used refer to exactly the same things. So accounts receivable (US) is the same as debtors (UK) and so on. Once again let's explain each item before we look at a realistic example.

What the company owns are called *assets*, and what the business owes are called *liabilities*.

Assets

Current assets
  Cash
  Accounts receivable
  Inventory

Fixed assets
  Tangible
  Intangible
  Long-term investments

Liabilities and shareholders' equity

Current liabilities
  Short-term borrowings
  Accounts payable

Long-term debt

Other liabilities

Shareholders' equity
  Issued stock
  Retained earnings

Figure 2.3 The balance sheet (US).

Assets
Fixed assets
  Tangible
  Intangible
  Investments
Current assets
  Stock
  Debtors
  Cash in hand and at bank
Creditors: amounts falling due within one year
Creditors: amounts falling due after more than one year
Provisions for liabilities and charges
Capital and reserves
  Called up share capital
  Share premium account
  Reserves
  Profit and loss account

Figure 2.4 The balance sheet (UK).

We group the assets by time considerations. *Current assets* are those which we are likely to turn into cash within the next 12 months:

- *Stock* (called inventory in the USA) is the stock of finished goods not yet sold or delivered. A manufacturer also includes work in progress and raw materials in its stock.

- *Debtors* which are mainly the amounts which customers owe for unpaid invoices.

- *Cash* which is the most liquid asset of all.

Assets which will give benefit over a longer term are called *fixed assets*. These are subdivided into *tangible* and *intangible*.

The tangible assets in a shop for example are the *furnishings and fittings*. In a factory there is *plant and machinery* and so on.

> **Smart things accountants may not tell us**
>
> In fact all the assets of a business do not, for various reasons, get on to the balance sheet. The people who work for the business are never on it, and things like brands likewise are often missed out. You would think that the right to produce a product called Mars Bars would have a value, but it is not on the balance sheet. Remember how difficult it was to value HAR. It had to have a value because of its experience and customer base, but this home-grown goodwill is also not on the balance sheet.

Smart test 11

If not all the assets are given a value on the balance sheet, how then do you give a value to a business?

Land and property can be different, since it is liable to appreciate in value. We may record that appreciation from time to time based on an independent valuation. Despite this, we still charge depreciation like any other asset.

Intangible assets are getting less common on balance sheets. There is a healthy suspicion of assets which are said to have a value but no substance. Goodwill, which arises on the purchase of a company, is probably an exception and you will certainly find this.

> **Creative accounting**
>
> If a company spends money on research and development (R&D) it has two ways of accounting for it. It can write it off against profits in the year the expenditure was made, or capitalize it. To capitalize it the company claims that the R&D work will have a value over many years. It should therefore be able to describe it as a fixed asset and depreciate it over time. This improves the short-term profit situation but mortgages the future since it will have to take the depreciation charge against profits during the following years.
>
> An aerospace company developing very expensive aircraft engines had a very high expenditure on R&D. It used this technique to disguise its profitability, did it for very large sums over very long periods, ran out of cash and went bust.

> **Creative accounting**
>
> Brand names, we have said, have a value that is often not expressed on the balance sheet. If the brand name has been purchased directly or by buying the company who owned the rights to it previously, it would seem fair to capitalize it and depreciate it over time. But if the brand is home grown it is like manufacturing money to capitalize it. You have sold products and made a profit on them by enclosing them in branded packages. You cannot add to that profit by then claiming that the asset has intangible value and should become an asset. This is now specifically forbidden by FRS 10.

The other common type of fixed asset comprise *trade investments*. These are investments in other companies which the board expects to be holding for the long term.

HAR Plc

In fact one of the problems that Andy has inherited is the capitalization of the company's database of clients and human resources. This is on the balance sheet with a value of more than £1 million. Lenders will probably not take this into account when they examine the credit-worthiness of HAR.

Think about the assets in your organization. It is smart to recognize what is the real value of an asset compared to what the accountants say. You might get better results from this knowledge.

Now let us turn to liabilities.

Once again the same definition occurs. Current liabilities are those liabilities which we will have to pay within the next 12 months. It is a strict definition. In fact balance sheets use the expression required by the company's act: "Creditors – amounts falling due within one year."

In this category we include:

- The *overdraft* which the bank can recall at any time.

- Any *short-term loans* which will have to be repaid within the next year.

- *Creditors* accounts payable, including the most important item "Trade creditors", are invoices outstanding.

- If we have announced a *dividend* but not yet paid it, it will be a current liability.

- *Tax* is a common item which we need to pay within 12 months.

So much for current liabilities. Long-term liabilities are also known as fixed liabilities. We can group them into long-term external liabilities, and liabilities to the shareholders. External liabilities include:

- *Long-term loans*

Creative accounting

It used to be common practice to make provisions so as to move costs from one period to another and thus smooth profit results. Provisions for repair work was a good example of this. FRS 12 forbids this type of provision except where there is already an obligation to pay money out, arising from an event before the balance sheet date.

In the past, directors could choose when to recognize a deferred tax liability. They were allowed to recognize only those liabilities they believed would actually crystallize. This gave them wide scope to massage the accounts. The new standard, FRS 19, which came into force early in 2002, replaced this old method with a new technique of full provision.

- *Provisions for liabilities and charges*: most balance sheets have an element of these which are liabilities which will probably have to be paid but not within a year. The most common example is deferred taxation. Other examples would be possible liabilities arising out of restructuring or legal actions.

That just leaves shareholders' funds and minority interests. Shareholders' funds normally have three elements:

- *Share capital* which is the nominal value of the issued shares. In the case of most UK shares, they are valued at a nominal 25 pence, in the US at par value $1. If, however, the board were to issue more shares to raise capital, it would sell them at somewhere near the current market value. The difference between those numbers is recorded as share premium. The Americans, slightly more plainly, call it "Moneys paid above par".

- The *reserves* or retained profits, as we have seen, also belong to the shareholders. They build up over time, and companies which have traded for a long time will have a lot of money in reserves. One item which must be shown separately is the "Profit and loss account", which is the total of past retained profits. Other reserves you might come across include the revaluation reserve which arises when assets are revalued.

- The final item is *minority interests*. This figure is similar to reserves. It records what part of the reserves belong to minority interests, i.e. profits which have been made by companies within the group which have other shareholders apart from the parent company which is presenting the report.

Once again the terminology will change according to the situation and the norms agreed by the finance director Here is the most recent published balance sheet for Compusell.

	2003 $m	2002 $m
Assets		
Current assets		
Cash and cash equivalents	3,360.9	2,309.8
Short-term investments	1,519.5	1,125.6
Accounts receivable	4,685.7	4,618.0
Financing receivables	1,142.9	844.4
Inventory	4,649.6	5,085.0
Other current assets	2,692.5	1,766.8
Total current assets	18,051.1	15,749.6
Property, plant and equipment, net	4,780.5	4,745.9
Long-term investments and other assets	4,309.0	3,375.9
Total assets	27,140.6	23,871.4
Liabilities and shareholders' equity		
Current liabilities		
Notes payable and short-term borrowings	936.1	921.8
Accounts payable	2,408.3	2,394.7
Employee compensation and benefits	1,329.3	1,295.5
Taxes on earnings	2,102.3	1,139.1
Deferred revenues	1,092.5	866.2
Other accrued liabilities	2,261.6	1,818.0
Total current liabilities	10,130.1	8,435.3
Long-term debt	1,551.1	2,374.4
Other liabilities	915.8	915.1
Commitments and contingencies		
Shareholders' equity		
Common stock at $1		
Amounts paid above par	1,545.1	892.5
Retained earnings	12,998.5	11,254.1
Total shareholders' equity	14,543.6	12,146.6
Total liabilities and shareholders' equity	27,140.6	23,871.4

To conclude the profit and loss and balance sheet, we would refer you to the "Notes to the accounts". These occur whenever you see the financial statements and give more detail or explanation of the items shown. In most cases they clarify matters, but they can be used actually to make things more obscure.

> **Creative accounting**
>
> We have seen that there are expenditures which must be taken now and reduce this year's profits. There are also expenditures which can be written off over time through depreciation. We also see provisions where good housekeeping makes the directors warn of impending expenditures. Why then do we need contingencies? But you will find them in the notes. The issue is "Does this item give full disclosure of the contingency?" and "Should it be a provision which would have the impact of reducing retained profits and thus shareholders funds?" Generally, a contingency is an obligation that may arise as a result of some future action not under the control of the company.

The cashflow statement

All managers look after the profit and loss account; smart managers understand the importance of the good management of a satisfactory cashflow. Ask any self-employed person and they will tell you that cashflow is what it is all about. It is harder to recognize this fact when you work for a large concern because, in most cases, cashflow is looked after by others, and it can seem to the people in the middle that there is an unlimited pot of cash to spend out there, and that a megacorp is always going to be able to spend up to its budgets.

In small companies the cashflow is a frequent (even daily) calculation as the firm tries to expand without running out of cash. But

> **Arthur Humphries, Managing Director, ICL**
>
> When briefing the training department about what he wanted them to include in a training programme for first- and second-line managers, "Look, in the end, try to make them spend the company's money as though it were their own." We shall see later just how smart that is.

even in large companies the cash position is an important issue in the company's ability to achieve its strategy.

Well-run companies make everyone aware of cash flow or set targets, such as how quickly managers have to get their customer invoices paid, which eventually end up assisting the company with its cashflow. Companies, as we have seen, do not necessarily go bust because they are not making profits; they go out of business, or get taken over, because they do not have the cash to pay their bills.

We have already noted the importance of the cash situation of a company which can be dramatically different from its profit situation. We saw how a company can be going bust profitably, and that it is essential for a chairman who is going to carry out his or her promises on dividend to have the cash as well as the profit to pay the amounts expected.

For middle managers the cashflow statement in the annual report is probably less important than the information they get in management accounts concerning cash, but we need to take a quick look.

Using fairly typical terms, the cashflow statement in an annual report looks like Figure 2.5.

Net cashflow from operating activities

The statement itself starts from the net cashflow from operating activities. You can normally tie this back to the profit and loss account but it takes a bit of effort using the reconciliation in the notes to the accounts. One of the main differences concerns depreciation. This figure lowers profits either through the cost of sales if the asset is used in the cost of the product, or in selling and distribution costs if the asset is, for example, to be used in distribution. But, of course, the cash to pay for them went out at the time they took

Net cash inflow from operating activities
Returns on investment and servicing of finance
Taxation
Capital investment and financial investment
Acquisitions and disposals
Equity dividends paid
Management of liquid resources
Financing
Increase/decrease in cash in the period
Reconciliation of net cash flow to movement in net debt

Figure 2.5 The cashflow statement.

delivery of the assets. So to reconcile this, the net cashflow adds back depreciation. This will be important when we get to investment appraisal in later chapters.

Returns on investment and servicing of finance

You are then told how much was paid and received in the servicing of finance, the interest paid and received.

Taxation

Now comes the next cash item – tax.

Capital expenditure and financial investment

This covers investment and disposal of fixed assets and trade investments.

Acquisitions and disposals

Where a company has taken over or sold the whole or a major part of a business, it shows the cash implication of that here. Later in the notes you get the detail of the balance sheet items which were bought or sold. Obviously this has an impact on the group balance sheet at the end of the year and could be very important in the case of a company which has a declared strategy of acquisition. Cash outflows are shown in brackets.

Equity dividends paid

This is the sum of dividends paid to its shareholders. There is usually a difference between the figure near the foot of the profit and loss account and this number. This is because the cashflow statement shows the dividends actually paid during the year, which will include the previous year's final proposed dividend, but exclude the current proposed dividend which will be paid out during the following year.

The profit and loss account records the dividends related to the current year profits irrespective of whether they have been paid.

We could have made the same point earlier with respect to interest paid and received, tax paid and capital expenditure. In every case the cashflow statement records the actual amount paid or received, whereas the profit and loss account records the amounts payable or receivable. Usually this is not terribly important, but it will be again when we come to investment appraisal where the cashflow is dominant in decision making.

Financing

This records the change in capital employed.

Increase/decrease in cash in the period

This is the bottom line of the cashflow.

Reconciliation of net cash flow to movement in net debt

This section explains in detail changes in net debt. Where you get this information, which is mandatory in the UK, it helps to link the cashflow to the balance sheet.

In conclusion, the cashflow statement gives an indication of the relationship between profitability and the ability to generate cash. As we have seen, profits without cash lead to ruin. Analysts will often develop models to assess the value of a company by reference to the present value of its future cashflows. The historical cashflow statement is useful in two ways. Firstly, analysts will be able to use cash information rather than just profit information in their models. Secondly, they will be able to use the historical cashflow to check the accuracy of previous predictions.

> **Smart challenge**
>
> Look at what you produce and sell. Do you understand whose profit and loss accounts your work impacts? Could you shine brighter if you made adjustments to how you do business and improve those figures? To further burnish your image, work out whether you make the best contribution you can to your organization's cashflow.

3 Understanding the Past

Introduction

This chapter deals with the financial ratios which people use at corporate level to compare last year with this year, and one business with another. So that we quickly get to the relevance and usefulness of such ratios, we will start with an overview of how four of the ratios offer the opportunity to get an impression of the financial status of a company. Following this, we will look at a benchmark or pattern for a company going through a 30-year lifecycle. We will see how the ratios change with time, and how the different stages of development appeal to different sets of investors.

An overview of four key ratios

Having looked at the key shareholder ratios in Chapter 1, we turn here to the key corporate ones. These are revealed in a company's annual report and talked about in the financial pages.

Senior managers are mainly interested in these ratios because they have a part in setting the share price, driving the strategy of the business and, of course, driving the financial part of the business plan. Andy McRae at HAR will give us a good example of this. Middle managers need to understand them as well since they will impact the

> **Smart test 12: looking back**
>
> What are the two key shareholder ratios available in the financial pages?

way they are asked to do their job. If you are asked to take an objective which is to do with profit margin, it is wise to know how such a ratio is calculated.

Company reports are notorious, of course, for what they hide as well as what they reveal. It is possible, at least in the short term, for creative accountants and their board-room masters to produce numbers which reflect more accurately their aspirations for the company rather than its actual performance. However, this does tend to disappear with time. As the business continues to perform in a certain way, so the accountants will eventually force the board to break bad news to the shareholders.

> **Smart rule of thumb**
>
> If a company has had to spend a lot of money on fixed assets before it can even start trading, e.g. Eurotunnel, return on assets will be an important measure of management performance.

Despite this caveat the annual report does give some very useable information. The most useful of the ratios are

- Capital gearing

- Income gearing

- Return on capital employed

- Pre-tax profit margin.

Armed with these four ratios you can start to understand the pres-

> **Market nervousness**
>
> Remember that share prices do not only depend on these corporate performance measures, the market frequently moves as a whole with all stocks gaining or losing at the same time. Uncertainty, whether it be in management's ability to achieve their plan, the strength of the dollar compared to the yen or political stability in Russia, always takes a toll on share prices.

sures on the board, and through them the pressures on the managers of the business. This is particularly true if you add a judicious reading of the chairman's statement.

We will give some examples of the ratios for Compusell and HAR, but it is probably worth your while to work at a real example relevant to you.

The four ratios below give an effective check on progress quite quickly. They are reasonably easy to calculate, and with practice take a matter of a few minutes to produce. Always do them for the two years in the report so that you can look at the change. You can then check the director's statements to see if they comment on changes which you regard as significant.

Frequently, the report will include "Facts for Shareholders" or

> **Attention to detail or what?**
>
> No document presented by a company gets more attention from directors and public relations people than the chairman's statement. It is carefully crafted to contain only the truth couched in a way which shows the chairman and the board in the best possible light.

"Five-year Record" which include some calculated ratios. The advantage of these is that they remove the need to do any calculations. Unfortunately there are two disadvantages to relying on these that make them much less useful than calculating them yourself.

> **Do it yourself**
>
> It is a smart idea to have a copy of the annual report of a company which you know quite well in reading the next part of the chapter. This gives you the opportunity to make sure you can work out the ratios, and to compare at least the differences between the two years in the report.

The first problem is that the published ratios are calculated in a way which suits each company. They will use figures which are not misleading or inaccurate, but which give a gloss on performance which the truly objective investigator wishes to avoid.

The second problem is connected. Companies use ratios which suit themselves and therefore do not use the same ones as others. So for the sake of consistency it is better to become very familiar with four ratios which you work out for yourself.

You can also build a personal database of examples which gives you various benchmarks for examining and comparing any company.

> **Keeping spirits up**
>
> Given the optimism/pessimism test about how well a company's finances are being managed, the chairman will always report the glass as being half full, rather than half empty.

This is particularly true if you study only one or a limited number of business sectors.

One final point of introduction. The rules of thumb quoted below are useful as you learn to appreciate the significance of the ratios. They are only guides, however, and we will see later how their significance varies depending on the business the company is in and the stage in its lifecycle it has reached.

Capital gearing

Shareholders' funds, or equity, include the money which the investors originally put into the company plus the profits which have been retained over the years. The debt involved here is the money owing on a long-term basis to banks and other financial institutions.

A private geared play

Suppose you buy a house for £130,000 with capital of £26,000 and a mortgage of £104,000. This gives the relatively high gearing of 80% debt and 20% equity. If the housing market does well, you may well find yourself in ten years' time living in a house worth £260,000, or double what you paid. The equity you have in it increases by considerably more than double even assuming you have made no repayments of capital. Your equity has gone up from £26,000 to £156,000, a six-fold increase. This is the positive side of gearing.

The downside of gearing is that you have to make regular interest payments and probably put some money aside each month to enable you to repay the mortgage at some time in the future.

The other downside is that just as your gain was exaggerated by gearing, so is any loss. If, as has happened in the UK housing market, there is a decline in prices over a number of years, then you lose. Take a decrease in value of 20% or £26,000 in your case and you have lost all your money. Worse than that and you hit so-called negative equity where the loan is higher than the value of the asset.

High gearing, where there is a lot of debt compared to shareholders' funds, involves using other people's money to make money for yourself. In fact most of us in our private lives have one high geared transaction from which, over time, we generally make a good profit: we own a house with a mortgage.

It is much like this in a business. Run at low gearing and you miss the opportunity to make money for yourself while using other people's capital, or run at high gearing and run the risk of profits lowered by interest charges and a cashflow strapped by repayment commitments.

When Andy looks at the figures for HAR he will want to compare last year with this year. He also has access to how things stand part way through the year he is presently in. This gives him the ability to understand thoroughly his gearing situation.

> **Capital gearing**
>
> Using the very simple ratio of long-term debt as a percentage of shareholders funds plus long-term debt:
>
> Low gearing is less than 10%
>
> Medium gearing is about 33%
>
> High gearing is about 66%
>
> It is common practice to refer to this ratio simply as "gearing".

HAR Plc

HAR has always been highly geared. The founders worked previously for another, much bigger organization. Seeing the huge potential for an up-market, technology-oriented recruitment agency they discussed the possibility of going on their own with their employers. They took a sympathetic view rather than showing them the door and a management buy-out was organized.

The founders put some of their own money in, the original company bought shares, but the bulk of the money came from a venture capital company which specialized in such situations.

In 2003 long-term debt was £2,040,000 and shareholders' funds £1,393,000, giving it a capital gearing ratio of 59%.

This was worse than the 2002 situation: long-term debt £1,153,000, shareholders' funds £1,485,000, giving capital gearing of 44%

Andy is further aware that if a balance sheet were raised now, a quarter into 2004, the situation would be worse still as long-term debt is now £3,013,000. If shareholders' funds stay the same at 1,393,000 – which is unlikely if the year shows a loss – capital gearing will be over 68%.

Compusell Inc.

How different is the position in Compusell. A major corporation with a strategy that always shunned loan capital, Compusell has over its many years of trading developed huge shareholders' funds from its retained profits.

Total shareholders' equity is 14,544, its debt at $1,551 is very low and its capital gearing ratio is 10%.

Income gearing

Income gearing tests the ability of a company to pay its interest bill out of its profits. Looking at the positive side of income gearing, you see the leveraging affect on profit again. Take the case of a company with income gearing of 60%:

Earnings before interest and tax	100
Interest payable	60
Profit for shareholders	40

See how the gearing affect exaggerates the effect of a modest rise or fall in profits. Here is the impact of earnings increasing by 10% and also decreasing by the same percentage:

	10% increase	10% decrease
Earnings before interest and tax	110	90
Interest payable	60	60
Profit for shareholders	50	30

In both cases the 10% change in earnings has had a 25% impact on the profit available for shareholders. This is known as financial leverage.

> **Income gearing**
>
> If you calculate the ratio as interest payable as a percentage of earnings before interest and tax:
>
> - Low gearing is less than 25%
>
> - Medium gearing is between 26% and 75%
>
> - High gearing is above 75%

As you would expect HAR spends 77% of its profits paying its interest bill, while Compusell needs about 5% to pay its.

Return on capital employed

The next two ratios in this overview are two profitability ratios. The first compares a number from the profit and loss account, profits before tax, with those items on the balance sheet which make up the

Understanding the Past

> **Smart test 13**
>
> If a company buys back some of its shares from its shareholders, does its gearing go up or down?

long-term capital used in the business. This long-term capital is made up of long-term liabilities and share capital.

Over time RoCE tells us what we need to know about the health of the company measured by profits. After all, the reason people put money into companies is so that managers use it to make return. If the managers cannot do it, then there are always bonds and banks that can.

> **Smart rule of thumb: return on capital employed (RoCE)**
>
> Calculated as net profit before tax divided by long-term capital:
>
> - Low profitability 0 to 10%
> - Medium profitability is between 10% and 20%
> - High profitability is above 20%

Compusell Inc.

Compusell's RoCE for 2003 was 18.1%. This was actually lower than 2002 (21.7%) although sales increased by some 10%. The chairman blamed pressure to keep prices down in a very competitive environment and the resultant lowering of the gross margin.

Pre-tax profit margin

This is a profit and loss account ratio. It compares the bottom line of the profit and loss account with the top line, profits with sales. It tells how much profit was earned for each dollar of sales. As we will see it is not only a corporate measure, but is one of the principle measures used when managers are running divisions and profit centres.

> **Smart rule of thumb: pre-tax profit margin**
>
> Calculated as net profit before tax as a percentage of sales revenues, it looks like this:
>
> - Low margin is below 2%
>
> - Medium margin is between 4% and 8%
>
> - High margin is above 8%
>
> Remember that all measures, and particularly this one, are highly dependent on the industry you are looking at. What is a poor margin for technology companies, for example, could be a very good one for a bookshop.

HAR Plc

HAR's profit margin last year was 1.5% and unless something is done will be a substantial negative figure this year. Andy does not know at this stage if the problem is more acute at the gross profit level or if the main concern should be indirect costs of selling, administration and overheads.

Looking for a benchmark

There is no such thing as a typical company. Its different products, markets and management styles make each enterprise unique. It is, however, possible to use the history of Compusell as a benchmark of the characteristics and ratios of a company over a long period of time.

The 30-year history of Compusell

Stage 1: inception to seven years old

Turn back the clock to the time when large mainframe computers were under attack from smaller more flexible minicomputers. At that time an electronics engineer created Compusell. The newly floated company had, in the early stages, the ability to generate very rapid growth of sales. The market is eager for the new computer concept, and the coowners, a venture capital company, are happy to put money into the new venture.

Compusell is very aggressive at this stage. It needs volume to cover its voracious appetite for cash as it invests millions of dollars in production infrastructure. This makes its competitiveness very sharp. It will, to a considerable extent, sacrifice profit for market share. It hires a salesforce of 'hunters', salespeople who enjoy the challenge of getting new business in fast. These salespeople are good at closing business and handling objections. If they do not close business fast, they go elsewhere.

> **Managing growth**
>
> Most would say that it is easier to run a company enjoying high growth of sales. The problem is to keep a contingency plan in mind if the growth falters for even a short period of time.

We should expect to find high morale in the company as business markets flock to the upstart.

Stage 1: the annual report

The chairman's statement. In the chairman's report we will expect to see a reflection of this growth, as indicated in these extracts:

"June saw another milestone when we shipped mini-computer number 100,000."

"Our sales growth last year exceeded 50%, and although this is likely to prove exceptional, Compusell is confident of its ability to take further advantage of the expanding market over the next few years."

The report's tone will reflect the excitement and enthusiasm of the fledgling, which is discovering success for the first time.

Stage 1: the ratios

The board is running Compusell by its cashflows rather than by its profit and loss account. It needs huge amounts of cash for capital investment and we expect to find very high levels of borrowing. This high gearing will show itself in both of the gearing ratios, with a high percentage of debt and very little profit left over once interest is deducted.

Profitability will be relatively low measured by both return on capital employed and the profit margin:

Compusell's ratios at stage 1

Gearing	75%
Income gearing	95%
RoCE	1%
Pre-tax profit margin	1%

Stage 1: the investors' ratios

Investors will find that the market only sees Compusell as having long-term potential in the high risk part of their portfolios. It is undesirable for the company to pay large amounts in dividend, since it needs all its cash to fund its expansion. So the yield will be low.

The P/E ratio will be very high as the market calculates future profit streams for the company as it gets into a position to exploit its assets. There is one other ratio to bring in here. Dividends are, we have said paid out of profit. It is useful to know what percentage of profit is needed to pay the dividend. The term we use is dividend cover which is the number of times the dividend is covered by the profits. If there is little left over having paid the dividend, the company may be starved of money for growth, or it may not be possible in the future to maintain the existing level of dividend. In this case Compusell's dividend cover may very well be high, not because the profits are huge but because the dividend is stingy.

Compusell's investor ratios at stage 1

Yield	0.3%
Price/earnings	35
Dividend cover	13

Stage 2: 7–15 years

Compusell has come of age. It has survived the heady days of 30% year-on-year growth and shown itself to be competitive. It has a viable market share in the areas where it already operates and is looking for new opportunities to make further investment either in new markets, such as overseas, or in new product areas such as personal computers.

This diversified growth will still cost a lot of money, but the business now generates a healthy cashflow and is profitable. There is still a

> **Venture capitalists**
>
> These entrepreneurs, often unit trusts or mutual funds, spread their bets around a lot of high risk start up businesses. That way they can afford the losses on the companies that don't make it, because when one like Compusell does succeed the venture capitalists make a lot of money.

fair amount of risk in the company. It is vulnerable to making mistakes as it moves into new activities. No matter how good the prospects, it is always more risky to take old products into new markets, or new products into old markets than to keep doing more of the same.

Stage 2: the annual report

The chairman's statement. We will expect now to see the chairman talking of some consolidation of its current affairs, although the emphasis of the report will still be on growth. Look for the new initiatives, as in the following extracts:

"Our earnings per share before exceptional items grew some 22%."

"Our strengthening financial position allows us to explore new countries seeking our products, whilst at the same time consolidating our strategy to focus on those parts of the world where we are already strong and where our returns will be the greatest."

Stage 2: the ratios

The debt ratios are still high. Almost certainly by this time the company will have been back to its investors for more cash through a rights issue. At this stage the venture capital shareholders will have taken some profits and reduced their holding. This, of course, radically reduces the debt to equity ratio, but it will rise again to reflect further borrowing to continue investment.

Profitability has improved to what could be described as fairly safe levels. This means that the current business will produce reliable profits, and it is only in the new areas of activity that there is still high risk.

Compusell's ratios at stage 2

Gearing	60%
Income gearing	75%
RoCE	10%
Pre-tax profit margin	4%

Stage 2: the investors' ratios

Compusell wants to pay out some dividend of real worth. It probably had to make promises in this area when it made its last cash call to shareholders and it sees dividend as a sign of impending "respectability". Nevertheless the yield is still well below the sector average, as the price of the share is buoyed by the market's expectation of further growth.

The P/E ratio is also still very high. It is probably less than other new entrants in stage 1 of their lifecycles, but it will be well above the industry average.

> **Rule of thumb warning**
>
> The Compusell example is valid when you compare the relative measures of, for example, P/E ratio. But the whole market fluctuates as well. So the rule of thumb has to be adjusted up or down depending on the general health of equities.

The dividend is stretching cover much more than in the first phase. Investors are starting to ask when the return to their money will start to come through, and there is no room for the very high dividend cover of the earlier stage.

Compusell's investor ratios at stage 2

Yield	1.6%
Price/earnings	25
Dividend cover	3.5

Stage 3: 15–23 years

The company has achieved respectability. The company is now well into the Standards and Poor 500 companies, the top 500 industrials measured by market share. It is a complex company now and the analysts are looking for good statements of strategy which prove that the current management can run a cruiser, having been very successful in managing fast patrol boats and destroyers.

> **Fitting the people to the job**
>
> At this stage the type of manager required to run the business is different from the original people who got it to this size. People who were at their best during the exciting start up and second phase may not be as competent in this bigger enterprise. Unless they can make the change they might be better to move on rather than become frustrated in an environment to which they are not entirely suited.

Its share price varies with the changes in the industry. A bad regulatory change, particularly in software bundling for example, could endanger profit growth significantly. Long-term planning is no longer a luxury, but a vital responsibility of the board and its advisers.

Compusell now has some 'big names' on its board with an ex-Senator among its numbers.

Risk has changed in its nature. The company could now afford to make some mistakes without threatening its actual life. The market sees the risk as comparative with other stocks in the sector. Investors see reports of sell-offs of one share in the sector and swaps into other companies in the same sector being recommended.

Stage 3: the annual report

It is unlikely that the annual report will claim that everything is rosy. Shareholders expect more circumspect statements with admissions of error and promises of remedy. A careful look at the ratios which the chairman chooses to report can be revealing. For example, if he produces a graph showing that the past 20 years of share price has consistently outperformed the market index, he is probably trying to reassure the market that there is still plenty of growth potential there. He does not want the growth in share price to stall, although it will certainly have slowed.

The chairman's statement. The follwing are examples of extracts from the chairman's statement for a stage 3 company:

"We see alliances with other companies as an important contributor to our vision to be the supplier of choice for people seeking high levels of features combined with international coverage."

"New technologies offer enormous opportunities to broaden the products and services available to our current customers. The internet will radically alter the way we conduct our lives."

"The reorganization which we completed during the year, has ensured that we can carry through our promises of presenting a global image and relationship with our key accounts world-wide."

Stage 3: the ratios

The ratios have now reached the mature end of industry averages. Gearing is at the low risk end and less than a third of profits are required to pay the interest bill.

The measure of return on capital employed is as meaningful and reliable as any other large company's, and reflects the sorts of return expected from the whole sector as opposed to the rapid growth part of the sector. The relatively high pre-tax profit margin shows the good profitability of the information technology sector:

Compusell's ratios at stage 3

Gearing	35%
Income gearing	30%
RoCE	20%
Pre-tax profit margin	8%

Stage 3: the investors' ratios

The dividend is an important part of large investors' portfolio plans. The yield will therefore tend to be around the average for the sector and even for the whole market. The P/E ratio is similarly near the average for the sector.

The dividend cover has gone sharply down as investors start to make the returns they were expecting at this stage in Compusell's lifecycle:

Compusell's investor ratios at stage 3

Yield	4%
Price/earnings	18
Dividend cover	1.9

Stage 4: over 25 years

The board is now commanding a battleship or a stately galleon. Shareholders have stopped looking for excitement in the share and want long-term promises on dividends and the delivery of these promises.

Compusell is in the Dow Jones 30 and has high-profile Chairman and non-executive directors. You will hear its chairman frequently on television and radio talking about the company's performance, the economic situation, the competitive environment and other current affairs. Using the naval example, it has now become a battleship.

> **Managing size**
>
> The battleship analogy holds true in the length of time it takes to get a large company to react to problems. Suppose the market for your products becomes more competitive and prices have to come down to maintain sales volume. To protect your bottom line you have to cut costs, either direct, the cost of making the product, or indirect, administration and overheads.
>
> A small business can make this happen immediately, whereas Compusell at this stage might take a year or more to make the correction, during which time we will see a lowering of the profit margin.

Representatives of the company now have a lot of power over standards bodies and supplier policies. Someone from Compusell is one of the panel in any debate with a computer context from virtual reality shopping to home working.

The sales force now has more "farmers" in it than "hunters". The company has well-founded key account management techniques in place to develop and protect marketshare. The third-party channels through which a large part of its sales go is encouraged by centrally worked out marketing promotions and offers.

At this stage the chairman sometimes complains about the view which the stock market takes of Compusell's shares. The company likes to think it is a growth and innovation enterprise, while the market sees it as primarily a seller of commodity products, with limited opportunities for the sort of growth which will make a significant difference to its profit stream.

> **The ability to obfuscate**
>
> As we will see in the next chapter, there is a continuing struggle between big businesses and the panels who set accountancy standards. The standards bodies' mission is to make companies give a "true and fair" picture of the affairs of the company.

Stage 4: the annual report

The chairman's statement. There is an emphasis on benefits to customers in the report. The company takes very seriously its dominant place in a number of markets and is anxious to show that it is not exploiting this. Compusell will boast of new offerings to its customers, lower prices and generally better service, as the extracts from the chairman's report show:

"Steady growth of sales, 4%, and earnings, 5.5%, demonstrate our progress towards meeting the expectations of both our shareholders and our customers."

"Against this economic and competitive background, Compusell's strategy remains clear. We will develop vigorously in our traditional markets and at the same time establish ourselves in new markets for our products and services both in our traditional areas and new parts of the world."

Stage 4: the ratios

The ratios are all safer than the industry average and are at the top end of the benchmark. There is no question in the short term that the company can maintain its market and profit growth, limited though that is. Investors will be wary for any signs of decline. Regulations and new competitors represent the biggest risk.

Compusell has already shown good control of costs, but this needs to be a continuing phenomenon to remain reflected in the profit margins:

Compusell's ratios at stage 4

Gearing	15%
Income gearing	20%
RoCE	25%
Pre-tax profit margin	10%

Stage 4: the investors' ratios

The share is now in almost all pension and private portfolios. The expectation is for dividend progress rather than capital growth, and the yield and dividend cover show it. The yield is well above the average and cover is at a low level. Dividend cover probably wants to stay around here except if there is an exceptional item affecting profits. The P/E ratio is the sign of the stately galleon.

Compusell's investor ratios at stage 4

Yield	5.9%
Price/earnings	13.8
Dividend cover	1.5

Here is a summary of Compusell's ratios over the four stages of its development. Whilst not a scientific benchmark, it provides a reasonable rule of thumb to make a preliminary judgement about any company. Look at the company's position in the stages of development, and then at its ratios. Look for inconsistencies with the benchmark and investigate from there.

Compusell's investor ratios

Compusell's ratios over the four stages

Gearing	75%	60%	35%	15%
Income gearing	95%	75%	30%	20%
RoCE	1%	10%	20%	25%
Pre-tax profit margin	1%	4%	8%	10%

Compusell's investor ratios over the four stages

Yield	0.3%	1.6%	4%	5.9%
P/E	35	25	18	13.8
Dividend cover	13	3.5	1.9	1.5

NB: This benchmark is viable when judged over the performance of companies and stock markets over many years. At the time of writing P/E ratios have been on average at a higher level and correspondingly yields lower. Time will tell if low inflation, and therefore relatively high P/E ratios are here to stay.

Conclusion

Whilst recognizing that all businesses, and indeed all sectors, have different characteristics, we can already see pigeon-holes which we can use to identify different kinds of companies. They require little working out but are very helpful in determining the health of a company.

Investors, for example, have different requirements for the shares in their portfolio. Suppose you are about to retire. You want to use your share portfolio to protect your capital, i.e. take little risk, and live on the dividends which the portfolio pays. In this case you will have a preponderance of stage 4 companies in your portfolio.

This is not true of young high-earners. They are paying income tax at the highest level and therefore do not need the dividend income. They are in no rush to turn the shares into cash and will therefore tend towards a portfolio of higher risk/higher return stage 1 companies.

Notice how easy it is to spot the type of company preferred if you have access to the three shareholder numbers and the four key ratios. To see how an inside senior manager looks at these ratios we turn to Andy McRae of HAR.

HAR Plc

We have seen the gearing problem at HAR. Extra borrowing was needed because of the drop in sales and margin. In the current year things have continued to go down. Here is a comparison between the ratios in 2003 compared with the first half of the current financial year.

	2003	Half year
Sales	10,284	4,628
Cost of sales	7,676	3,692
Gross profit	2,608	936
Gross margin	25%	20%
Expenses	1,925	885
EBIT	683	51
Interest	526	352
Profit before tax	157	−301
Profit margin	1.5%	−6.5%

Andy sees the decline into loss and the slight decrease in gross margin. Another figure he works out is the ratio of fixed costs, expenses, compared to the gross profit. In 2003 this was 74% and has become 95% this year. In other words, his fixed costs are getting worse in relation to the sales and profit he is making.

Becoming familiar with financial information

To become really familiar with these numbers you need to have a look at a few companies. If you do not already have them, you need to acquire a number of annual reports. There are two main ways that you can do this. The first is to ring up or write to the companies themselves. In most cases the switchboard operator will understand your request and either put you through to someone in shareholder relations who will take your name and address, or the operator will take your name and address. Do not forget that the annual report is for most companies part of their promotional material and they are happy enough to disseminate them. For the addresses and telephone numbers you will need a guide, such as a good company guide to tell you the head office. This is available in most reference libraries.

Alternatively, you can use the FT Annual Reports service. Look at the stock market reports at the back of the Companies and Markets section. Where you see in the Notes column an ace of clubs, this refers to the fact that the company is a member of this service. At the bottom right of the right-hand page you will see the explanation. You need to ring a number and place your order. They will then send you a copy of the report by return. The authors have used the service many times and it has worked well. It is now available on-line at www.icbinc.com.

> **Smart summary and challenge**
>
> Choose a business sector that you wish to study. From the financial pages try to identify by using the P/E ratio and yield four companies which could fit into the four-stage model proposed in this chapter. Get hold of the reports for these companies and calculate the four key ratios. You should see correlation among all these numbers and the four stages of growth. Where you see inconsistency try to explain it.

4 Analysing the Past

Introduction

The ratios given in the previous chapter are a smart guide to the main health of a business. There are, of course, many more. For some readers Chapter 3 may be enough on the topic of ratios at corporate level, and they may wish to continue to Chapter 5 which moves into management accounts – the financial and other performance measures that managers look at further down the business. This chapter gives more detail about the ratios in Chapter 3 and explains further ratios of interest to the shareholder and in many cases as a toolkit for middle managers. If, for example, one of your performance measures concerns return on assets, days used to collect debt or inventory turnover, then it might be useful to continue to the end of the chapter. If you are paid by results it is smart to know how the umpire is going to calculate the score.

A model of the ratios derived from an annual report

Spreadsheet 4.1 has all the items from the HAR profit and loss account and balance sheet that we need to calculate all the detailed ratios. You should be able to identify each of these items from any annual report you are examining. There is one notable exception to this rule. In US reports there is no legal requirement to state the

Company name: HAR Plc
Currency and units: £000's

Spreadsheet 4.1

		Year	1999 £000's	1998 £000's		Year	1999 £000's	1998 £000's
Total sales turnover	A		10,284.0	13,856.0	Trade creditors	K	680.0	465.0
Profit before taxation	B		157.0	2,078.0	Short term loans	L	473.0	251.0
Interest payable	C		526.0	280.0	Total current liabilities	M	2,890.0	2,616.0
Depreciation	D		152.0	91.0				
					Long term loans	N	2,040.0	1,153.0
Tangible fixed assets	E		983.0	780.0	Provisions	O	0.0	0.0
Intangible fixed assets	F		1,096.0	240.0	Other long term liabilities	P	0.0	0.0
Other fixed assets	G		0.0	0.0				
					Total shareholders' funds	Q	1,393.0	1,485.0
Stocks	H		0.0	0.0	Minority interests	R	0.0	0.0
Trade debtors	I		3,027.0	3,580.0				
Total current assets	J		4,244.0	4,234.0	Average no of employees	S	49	52
					Total emp remuneration	T	1,248.0	1,260.0

Calculated figures follow

		1999	1998			1999	1998
Tan+Intan fixed assets	AA	2,079.0	1,020.0	Quick assets	FF	4,244.0	4,234.0
Total assets	BB	6,323.0	5,254.0	Total debt	GG	2,513.0	1,404.0
Total liabilities	CC	4,930.0	3,769.0	Tangible net worth	HH	297.0	1,245.0
Net assets	DD	3,433.0	2,638.0	Pre-interest profit	II	683.0	2,358.0
Capital employed	EE	3,433.0	2,638.0	Net working capital	JJ	1,354.0	1,618.0

Spreadsheet 4.1

remuneration of employees. For this reason most reports exclude it. In that case you will not be able to calculate one of the employee ratios. Spreadsheet 4.2 has the ratios calculated for HAR Ltd. Spreadsheet 4.3 has the same data for Compusell, and Spreadsheet 4.4 the ratios for Compusell.

We will look at the detailed ratios in six groups:

- Growth
- Profitability
- Liquidity
- Asset utility
- Gearing
- Employee

Analysing the Past 93

Company name:
HAR Plc

Profitability	1999	1998
Return on capital employed	4.6%	78.8%
Profit margin	1.5%	15.0%
Return on assets	2.5%	39.6%
Shareholders' return	52.9%	166.9%

Gearing	1999	1998
Capital gearing	59.4%	43.7%
Income gearing	77.0%	11.9%

Liquidity		
Current ratio	1.5	1.6
Quick ratio (Acid test)	1.5	1.6

Employee ratios in round numbers		
Sales per employee	209,878	266,462
Profit per employee	3,204	39,962
Average wage per employee	25,469	24,231

Asset utility		
Stock turnover		
Collection period	107.4	94.3
Asset turnover	162.6%	263.7%

Growth rates	
Sales growth	-25.8%
Profit growth	-92.4%

Spreadsheet 4.2

Company name:
Compusell Inc
Currency and units: $m

Year		1999	1998		Year		1999	1998
		$m	$m				$m	$m
Total sales turnover	A	35,384.2	32,251.9	Trade creditors	K	2,408.3	2,394.7
Profit before taxation	B	3,075.9	3,349.6	Short term loans	L	936.1	921.8
Interest payable	C	176.7	161.7	Total current liabilities	M	10,130.1	8,435.3
Depreciation	D	1,405.3	1,169.9				
				Long term loans	N	1,551.1	2,374.4
Tangible fixed assets	E	4,780.5	4,745.9	Provisions	O	0.0	0.0
Intangible fixed assets	F	0.0	0.0	Other long term liabilities	P	915.8	915.1
Other fixed assets	G	4,309.0	3,375.9				
				Total shareholders' funds	Q	14,543.6	12,146.6
Stocks	H	4,649.6	5,085.0	Minority interests	R	0.0	0.0
Trade debtors	I	4,685.7	4,618.0				
Total current assets	J	18,051.1	15,749.6	Average no of employees	S	93,684	91,654
				Total emp remuneration	T		

Calculated figures follow

		1999	1998				1999	1998
Tan+Intan fixed assets	AA	4,780.5	4,745.9	Quick assets	FF	13,401.5	10,664.6
Total assets	BB	27,140.6	23,871.4	Total debt	GG	2,487.2	3,296.2
Total liabilities	CC	12,597.0	11,724.8	Tangible net worth	HH	14,543.6	12,146.6
Net assets	DD	17,010.5	15,436.1	Pre-interest profit	II	3,252.6	3,511.3
Capital employed	EE	17,010.5	15,436.1	Net working capital	JJ	7,921.0	7,314.3

Spreadsheet 4.3

Growth

One of the first things you do when looking into an annual report is to examine the growth of sales and compare this to the growth of pre-tax profit. This is a good overall indicator of the progress the business made during the last 12 months. Without growth it is difficult for any business, no matter what industry it is in, to have a long-term future.

> **Gary Hamel, London Business School academic**
>
> Companies should measure their success not by the fact they are still around and making money, but by how many opportunities they missed.

Gary Hamel has a point, but you still need to look at a company in the context of its industry. A food retailer is unlikely through normal trading to have the same sales growth as a company in the technology business at this time. The question is: "Is the company getting as much growth in its sales as comparable companies in the same business?"

The other pointer we get from the two growth ratios is if profit growth is keeping up with sales. Anyone who has been in a small company will know how it feels to, say, double sales, with all the problems and work that that entails, only to realize that in the same period profits have stayed the same or even gone down. Of course, from time to time sales growth may precede profit growth where a company has put resources and money into new markets or new products, but in the end profit growth has to catch up.

HAR and Compusell

On this measure HAR is in trouble. Its sales have declined by 26% from last year, and its profits by 92% – another proof that it was ready and resourced for an expansion that did not occur.

Compusell has achieved nearly 10% growth, but with a decline in profitability. We will need to look at the actual profit ratios to discover whether this is serious or not.

Profitability ratios

Companies are in business in the final analysis to make profits. Note, however, David Packard's wise pronouncement.

> **David Packard, computer company founder**
>
> One of our most important management tasks is maintaining the proper balance between short-term profit growth and investment for future strength and growth.

Here are the four most commonly used ratios to indicate to managers, shareholders and employees how well their business is doing in terms of profitability.

Return on capital employed (RoCE)

The smart manager finds this a key indicator of managerial performance. The point is that shareholders have given them the use of their money in preference to earning interest in a safer savings scheme. Managers have to use that money to produce a greater return. Not only a greater return now, but the ability to reinvest in order to produce growth of return. This figure tells us if they are doing this. It is a good guide as to whether sufficient return is being generated to maintain and grow dividends from increasing profits and cashflow.

We have seen that this is considered to be the main indicator of the profitability of a business. After all, the basis of enterprise is to take money in the form of share capital and loan capital and use it to earn profits. (Capital employed is the sum of shareholders' funds, long-term liabilities, provisions and minority interests. In the model N + O + P + Q + R.) This percentage is a good guide to the performance of managers in producing sufficient return. A sudden alteration for better or worse will give rise to further investigation to see what has changed.

> **Smart test 14**
>
> If a company pays off some long-term debt, what happens to its return on capital employed?

Earlier we gave some examples, in terms of a simple rule of thumb, of what might be called high, medium or low return. The real usefulness, however, comes in first of all comparing previous years' performance against the most recent historical figures and secondly comparing performance against other companies in the same business. Return on capital employed is important whatever the industry you are looking at.

Many people regard it as the key profitability ratio and the definition we give here is the one used by most commentators:

Return on capital employed = net profit before tax/capital employed.

Profit margin

This shows the profits made per pound (or dollar) of sales. This is a smart ratio because we can adjust it easily. Suppose we want to understand the impact of higher interest rates on a company, we can simply recalculate this ratio. As businesses grow, their managers are concerned over time to maintain a good "bottom-line profit margin". It is quite reasonable that peaks and troughs will occur. For example, where a company has been involved in a major expansion, it may take some time, measured in years, to get back to its original profit margin and then exceed it.

It is, of course, deeply bound up with the gross margin, which is the ratio of the gross profit to the total sales turnover. When there are concerns about the bottom-line profit margin, we will have to look at the gross margin to see if the problem lies there or whether it is the indirect costs which are at fault. We will also read carefully what the managers say in explanation of any change or shortcoming.

Profit margin = net profit before tax/sales revenue.

Return on assets

This ratio is more important in some industries than others. Basically the clue is the amount of investment in fixed assets required to create a going concern. In a firm of consultants, for example, where there are few fixed assets since arguably the main assets are the people acting as consultants, this ratio will have little relevance.

> **Telephone operators**
>
> Good examples of a business where return on assets is important are the telephone operators. Before they are able to make money from selling the use of the telephone, they have to lay out massive amounts of investment money to create the network in the first place. In such cases managers will be very interested in the subsequent efforts of their people to squeeze profits out of these assets. "Make the assets sweat" is the battle cry of a managing director who has spent a lot of capital in an enterprise.

If you take the case of a well-established company with little debt on the balance sheet, its performance in terms of return on capital employed may have become stable and reasonable. A better test of its ability to continue this into the future may very well be to examine its performance against assets. Indeed, if you can get close enough to a company to find out how its bonus scheme works, you may find that directors and/or staff are paid by the profit made on assets.

Return on assets = net profit before tax/total assets.

In cases where this measure is important, the board will frequently report on it in the annual report. If the calculation you have made does not exactly correspond with what the report states, check which measure of profit the company has used. In this model we use profit before tax since tax is not entirely within the control of managers and may differ wildly from year to year depending on circumstances. Sometimes the annual report will use net profit after tax in any of the profitability calculations we are discussing. Some calculations use earnings before interest and tax (EBIT), another frequently used profitability term. Once again, nobody said life was easy.

> **Smart test 15**
>
> If a company moves to outsourcing for its information technology requirements and sells the computer equipment it owns to the outsourcing company, what is the impact on its return on assets?

Compusell Inc.

Compusell has more than $9 billion dollars in fixed assets, and $27 billion when you add in current assets. On this it is making a return of 11.3%. It may, however, be concerned that this measure has declined further than return on capital employed. Maybe this company, too, was prepared for higher growth in sales than it achieved.

Put simply, companies using their assets efficiently will have a relatively high return compared to less well run businesses.

Return on shareholders' funds

This ratio measures management's ability to use the share capital in the business efficiently and produce good returns. There is a tendency to use this measure as a final measure of profitability. In some ways it is a more logical measure of return than RoCE, since the latter ratio is lowered by the inclusion of loan capital in capital employed. Some would argue that because the interest on loan capital has already been deducted from net profit before tax, then the providers of the loan capital have already had their return and should be excluded from the capital employed. That is the case with this ratio calculated as follows:

> Return on shareholders' funds =
> net profit before tax/total shareholders' funds less intangible assets.

> **Smart rule of thumb**
> We would expect a return of 10% to give room for the payment of tax and dividends and retain enough profits in the business to fund its growth.

In a small business, you could even use this measure to see whether it is worthwhile being in business at all. If a small business cannot produce, say, 5% return on shareholders' funds, then the owners might as well put the money into a building society where it will, of course, be much more secure.

HAR and Compusell

All of Compusell's profit ratios are very positive, and shareholders can have no complaint about the short term. But remembering David Packard's dictum above, they may well look for reasons for the decline in profitability in the annual report, and, more importantly, actions which the board is going to take to protect long-term profitability.

HAR seems to have a very high return on shareholders' funds. However, do not forget the way we calculate this ratio. There is a high level of intangible asset in the HAR accounts. If you take a very wary view of such assets it is safer to drop them. If you drop them, as we do in this ratio, then you have to reduce shareholders' funds by that amount. This takes shareholders' funds to only £297,000, which means that the return is very high relative to the new figure.

Liquidity ratios

Sometimes known (not technically accurately) as solvency ratios, liquidity ratios demonstrate a company's ability to meet short-term obligations.

> **Can you pay your bills?**
>
> Take a simple business – a jobbing builder. If you ask the average jobbing builder what their liquidity ratios are like, you may very well get a glazed look and no reply. If, however, you ask them what their customers owe them, what they owe their suppliers, how much they have in the bank, or more likely how much they owe the bank, and when their next tax bill is due, they will almost certainly know the answers to a reasonable accuracy off the top of their heads. This is the basis of the liquidity ratios.
>
> They are, for example, well aware that if they fail to complete a job, having bought the materials for the whole job and finished 90% of it, they will not get paid. If there is a delay in payment, they in turn will have difficulty in paying their suppliers. If they do not pay their suppliers, they will immediately stop supplying them. Similarly if there is a delay in getting cash in, they will not be able to pay their people who will equally quickly stop working for them. So they keep careful tabs on the "liquidity" in their businesses.

Current ratio

This ratio shows how well the current assets, assets which will be turned into cash in the next 12 months, cover the current liabilities, debts or obligations which must be paid in the next 12 months. If the ratio is, for example, 1.5, it means that for every £1 outstanding to be paid within a year, there is £1.50 in assets due to become cash quickly. You calculate the ratio by dividing current assets by current liabilities.

Remember always that it is management's job to move working capital round the business cycle as quickly as possible. This means that managers want to keep working capital to a minimum, provided always that they do not get into short-term trouble with their creditors by becoming known as bad payers.

Large businesses therefore will run with a current ratio near to or even below 1. In the case of a company such as one which owns a chain of pubs and restaurants, they may very well work with a ratio of less than 1. The fact that they can rely on large amounts of cash coming into the business on a daily basis means that there is no danger that they will be unable to meet short-term obligations even though at any point in time the working capital ratio is less than 1. If the cash business works with stock which they pay for after it is sold this situation will certainly arise.

> **Big brother**
>
> Some companies also have a great deal of power over both their customers and their suppliers. Consider a telephone operator. If a customer goes into arrears the company can quickly turn off the service and then charge a fee for turning it on again once the account has been regularized. There is not much the customer can do. Changing to another supplier of service will be difficult if they have a poor record of payment. This means that the credit collection period is pretty quick for a telephone operator.
>
> Its relationship with its suppliers also gives it great liquidity advantages. If a telephone company chooses to make a supplier wait an extra few days before making payment, there is little the supplier, who needs the volume business available, can do except wait. From these facts alone it is not surprising that the large telephone operators have current ratios well below 1. In effect the company's credit period, the amount of time measured in days it takes to collect money from debtors (see below), is shorter than its opposite, the company's settlement period. The settlement period is the amount of time the company takes to pay its creditors.

Our jobbing builders, on the other hand, probably have to have working capital, including access to short-term lending, which gives a ratio of say 1.5. This gives them the cover against problems and ensures a continuation of their ability to pay the wages and get supplies. Simply put, the higher the ratio, the higher the security that the company has sufficient cashflow for its short-term obligations.

Quick ratio or acid test

The value of stock is normally held at the lower of what the items cost and what they could be sold for. This should give a reasonably sensible statement of the value of the stock. But, of course, in order to turn stock into cash you have to complete the work in progress and sell the finished goods. Company watchers therefore apply a more stringent liquidity test than the working capital ratio by taking stock out of the equation. This quick ratio, or acid test, is that more stringent test.

> **When is an asset not an asset?**
>
> A way to remember that there can be a huge difference between what the figures say and what the physical reality is, is the old story of the jobbing builder who claimed to his bank manager, through his balance sheet, to have a fixed asset of a cement mixer and a stock of cement. In fact when the bank manager visited the premises and looked around he found that the cement mixer had in it hardened concrete. Whilst the balance sheet was accurate, the truth was that neither the fixed asset nor the cement held in stock had any value at all.

The importance of the working capital ratios to smaller companies is often made greater by their bank's willingness to lend being dependent on their maintaining an agreed level of liquidity. A bank may, for example, limit its overdraft facility to a small company to say 80% of its outstanding debtors. Or it could refuse facilities where the current ratio has fallen below 1.

HAR and Compusell

Despite its being a huge company, Compusell keeps a high level of liquidity. HAR does as well, but we know that its liquidity must be threatened by its increasing debt, and therefore interest payments. Its direct, indirect and interest expenses run to £10 million a year, or £850,000 per month. From the 2003 profit and loss account we know that sales were also running at about £850,000 per month. The difference between current assets and current liabilities is £1.354 million. If sales fell by half, then in less than four months it will have used up all its working capital, i.e. its current ratio would be down to 1 and still falling.

Asset utility

In the section on profitability we emphasized the importance of the managers of a business producing a satisfactory return on the money which shareholders and lenders have put in. The other crucial measure of the performance of management is to see how well they are "sweating the assets".

There are three key business ratios involved in this measurement.

Stock turnover

In an ideal world a company would buy in or manufacture finished goods just before they are due to be delivered to customers. This minimizes the cost of holding the stock in warehouses and, of course, reduces the requirement for working capital.

We can measure this from the report and accounts by dividing the sales by the current stock. This tells us how many times in a year the stock has been turned over. In simple terms, the more times management have turned over its stock the better.

You will sometimes see stock turnover expressed in days. Sales divided by stock gives the number of times stock was turned over in the year. If you divide 365 by stock turnover you get the average

> **Don't compare apples with chairs**
>
> Stock turnover is, of course, very much dependent on the type of business that the company is in. We would expect a supermarket to turn over its stock very quickly compared, say, with a manufacturer of aeroplanes. In the latter case the length of time the eventual product is work in progress, i.e. is being built, is bound to be lengthy and therefore its stock turnover quite low. If you take a greengrocer, some of whose products become unsellable within a few days of arriving in stock, you could expect a stock turnover of as much as 40 times per year. A company selling heavy engineering goods may well be satisfied with 4 or 5 times.

number of days stock was held. So a stock turnover of 10 times a year could also be expressed as "Average time stock is held = 36.5 days".

The calculation described here is a convenient one since the accounts will always show the figure for sales turnover and stock. A more accurate measure of stock turnover is obtained by using the figure for cost of sales rather than turnover. This may be available in the annual accounts and if so should be used. The calculation we have used is the more common.

The internal performance measures used by a company would provide a more accurate measure of stock holding efficiency by using the figure for cost of sales rather than the turnover figure. They would also look at stock turnover product by product. Depending on the gross margins on the various products this could give a different picture from the one available to the public. This is simply another example where the managers of the company are better informed than the public and where they use such information for planning purposes. We should be conscious of the problem and look out for

Smart test 16

A warehouse manager who keeps a lot of obsolete stock will have a better or worse turnover ratio as a result. Which is it?

where this could be significant. For example, the group accounts of a conglomerate would combine a variety of types of business that would result in the stock turnover being averaged and in itself not a useful figure.

HAR and Compusell

Since HAR carries no stock this is not a relevant measure. In the case of Compusell its performance at 7.6 (last year 6.3) is probably at least average for the industry, and showed an improvement of 20%.

Collection period

Another crucial measure of management efficiency is the amount of time it takes to get money in, calculated by: debtors divided by average daily sales. A poor performance, of say 110 days, probably shows that there is a problem in the company's business systems. It could, of course, be even more problematical if the real reason for delay is disputed amounts, where the customer does not agree with the figure on his or her bill, or unmet expectations for delivery, where the customer is disputing whether the supplier has delivered what was promised.

In technology shares, a high collection period often arises as a result of the supplier having to spend time to make the product work to the customer's satisfaction.

Compusell

In view of Compusell being in the technology sector, collecting money in 48 days on average is very good. The consumables side of the business, which has high volumes and good control over poor payers, probably helps it. It probably also puts a lot of effort into vetting for their credit-worthiness the resellers it chooses to use as a distribution channel. They do have the ability, after all, to stop supplying resellers who pay persistently late. They will also have various rewards and bonuses for prompt payment.

Beware of doing this calculation for companies that do a lot of trade in cash. If, say, 50% of its income comes with no collection period at all, because the customer pays cash, then we should take that number out of the calculation to find the real collection period. Once again, inside the company where they have the necessary information they probably set middle management collection targets taking cash sales into account. An outsider may be unable to do better than look at the total sales figure since we do not know how much was done in cash. This does not invalidate the calculation entirely since we can compare the performance of management this year to last year, and we can compare the company with other companies in the same industry.

> **Smart rule of thumb: collection periods**
>
> If you are looking at an industry where normal payment terms are 30 days, then you should expect the collection period to be around 50–70 days. Less is a good performance, more reveals a likely problem.

Asset turnover

We have said that shareholders have given the managers of the business capital on which to earn a return. They have also given them an asset base to work with. A simple measure of their efficiency in using these assets is to compare the asset base with the total sales turnover. You calculate this by dividing total sales turnover by total assets.

HAR and Compusell

Compusell's asset turnover at 130% is what you might expect. This ratio has no relevance for HAR, which has very few fixed assets and most of these are intangible. HAR's main assets are its people and, as we know they are not a balance sheet item, although they will be taken into account when valuing the business.

> **Smart rule of thumb: asset utilization**
>
> Differing as usual by industry, asset utilization is high at the retail end of the spectrum, at say more than 250%, and low in property letting, at say 20%.

Gearing

To recap, gearing compares the amount of the company's external liabilities with the amount of money in shareholders' funds. High gearing carries a number of implications for companies and shareholders. If the company has a high level of debt compared to shareholders funds, it is of course vulnerable to increases in interest rates. Whereas income gearing, or interest cover, may be satisfactory at the time the loans were taken out, such a ratio may become dangerous if interest rates go up sharply. Such potential change should be taken into account when judging a company's gearing.

Low gearing is not in itself always a wholly positive sign either. If a company has little or no debt, shareholders may wonder if management is doing all it can to expand the business and take the well-informed risks which go with higher returns. Low gearing gives the potential, however, for borrowing if good opportunities arise. We need to ask ourselves if a low-geared company is becoming poised to raise money from lenders, for example, to make an acquisition. Watching the financial pages will give this information particularly when a company you are interested in is reporting annual or half-yearly figures. Around that time the company's strategy will be announced and commented on in the financial pages.

The capital gearing ratio

This ratio, as we have seen, is a comparison of the long-term debt of a company with its net shareholders' funds. The higher the ratio, the more likely it is that debt will become a burden. The more debt, the more interest, the lower the profits and therefore the potential for paying dividends is threatened. The calculation is long-term debt, as a percentage of net shareholders' funds plus debt.

HAR Plc

By this calculation the capital gearing ratio is 59%.

Some people would be more conservative than this, and take net shareholders' funds as total shareholders' funds minus intangible assets. On this measure HAR looks even more vulnerable than we assessed in Chapter 3. It has more than £1 million in intangible assets. This reduces its tangible net worth to £297,000 and with long-term debt at £2,040,000 this adjusted capital gearing ratio is 87%.

This adjusted capital gearing ratio can be an important one in determining the credit-worthiness of a company and its potential to grow the business by borrowing further money.

Lenders are less likely to lend to companies with a high level of intangible assets. Don't forget that they tend to look in the first place

---

Creative accounting

Companies also, despite FRS 5, have scope for keeping some of their assets "off balance sheet". The example of an operating lease allows the company to have the use of the asset without declaring ownership. Thus neither the asset, nor the liability to the leasing company, appears. This makes the amount of debt look lower than it actually is.

FRS 4 stopped another piece of creative accounting in this area. There is a type of share called a convertible. This starts life very much like a loan with a regular interest payment due on the amount put in as convertible share capital. The shareholder, however, has the right to convert it into ordinary shares at some point in the future. Companies who wanted to lower their capital gearing ratio chose to put convertibles into the equity part of the equation somewhat too early.

for security, and they know that intangible assets may have little or no value in the event of a forced sale.

A profitable company, however, can normally retain part of its earnings, after dividends, to help fund its growth and invest for the future. This addition to shareholders' funds allows the company to borrow more without increasing its gearing ratio. Acceptable gearing ratios, as usual, vary from one industry to another, but it is possible to suggest a rule of thumb.

> **Smart rule of thumb**
>
> Take a company with debt and equity, which totals £100 million. Here are three examples of how that might be held.
>
> | | | | |
> |---|---|---|---|
> | Debt | 10 | 33 | 66 |
> | Equity | 90 | 67 | 34 |
> | Capital gearing ratio is therefore | 10% | 33% | 66% |
>
> The rule of thumb has these numbers as low, medium and very high.

The income gearing ratio

This ratio indicates the company's ability to service its debt. It is the ratio of interest payable to the profits out of which interest is paid. It takes a bit more working out than the other ratios discussed because the figures you need may be in the notes to the accounts rather than on the profit and loss account itself. It has, however, the merit of being impossible to fudge. Nowadays many people regard it as the key gearing ratio. Calculate the ratio as interest payable divided by net profit before interest and tax.

This ratio highlights the profits available to pay gross interest. It shows how easily interest can be paid out of profits and, therefore, indicates the possibility of the company getting into problems in paying its interest in the future. If a company has a good record of profits and there is an obvious upward trend in profitability, this ratio may be more useful than the previously mentioned gearing ratio.

For example, a management buyout may be highly geared at the outset as the managers borrowed the money to buy the company. A strong profit trend and an improving income gearing should satisfy shareholders and even give scope for further borrowing if that is appropriate within the announced strategy. This assumes that the growth potential is still there. At some point the shareholders and board will probably prefer to pay down debt and increase the number of shares. At that time the gearing will obviously fall.

> Given Compusell's low gearing, we must ask whether it is really taking advantage of the growth in the market. Could they make more sales and profits if they borrowed more money?

You can easily see from this how much less risk to lenders and shareholders alike there is in the low geared company where the profits cover the interest paid. It is a very different story in the case where interest is 80% of profits. There is not much room left here to pay tax and dividends, and if profits were to dip slightly or interest rates go up a touch, then income gearing could easily rise to above 100% and the existence of the company become threatened. Remember the gearing example in Chapter 3.

Smart rule of thumb

Low income gearing is 20%   Medium 50%   High 80%

Employee ratios

So far we have studied the hard data revealed in the company report from a balance sheet and profit and loss account angle. There is one

Analysing the Past   111

> **Creative accounting**
>
> We saw earlier how companies can capitalize their research and development costs. It is also possible to capitalize the finance costs incurred when borrowing to finance the construction of fixed assets. The cost of the asset when it goes on to the balance sheet is taken as its cost plus finance costs. This can have the affect of obscuring interest cover because the charge shown on the profit and loss account for interest is reduced by the interest that has been capitalized. It also means that the asset, at least at the outset, could be on the balance sheet at a higher value than market value. This problem is lessened by FRS 11.

other important area to be looked at which is the people who work for it, often called "our greatest asset" in the chairman's statement. We need to see how well comparatively the company is using this great asset by looking at some productivity and remuneration ratios.

> **Smart test 17**
>
> Many annual reports do not give the average number of employees for the year, but rather the employees at year end. If last year a company had 850 employees at year end and 660 the year before, what would you use as the average number of employees for last year?

Sales per employee

There are big variations between different industries, with labour-intensive industries such as services much lower than well-mechanized manufacturing such as the computer industry. Hotels could well run with half the sales productivity of electronic manufacturers.

> **Smart rule of thumb**
>
> The hotel industry with its high level of staff giving customer service may be less than $80,000 sales per employee and electronic manufacturing with its high level of automation $400,000 or even more.

If a company is falling behind its competitors in sales per employee, it could very well lead to a reduction in profit. People are expensive both to keep and to make redundant, so companies look carefully at this ratio to ensure they are keeping up their competitive edge, or at least not losing ground.

Profit per employee

If a company has a competitive sales per employee figure, but a lower than average profit per employee, we may feel that its costs – direct or indirect – are not under as good control as those of its competitors.

> **Smart rule of thumb**
>
> The construction industry needs a lot of people to build its products. Such companies might run with profit per employee of, say, $6,000 or less. In the property-letting business it is the assets that do the work and profits per employee could be 10 times that.

HAR Plc

The problems of HAR show up again in relation to the employee ratios. It does quite well in terms of the sales per employee figure of £209,878, but we should expect this since each consultant will add a lot of value. When they place a person the firm is well rewarded. You will see the collapse of profit per employee from last year to this. Notice, too, its average wage per employee, which, understandably, is also very high.

Lack of competitiveness in profit per employee is a signal to the board to review the number of people it employs. Such a situation will have to be countered by increasing sales and improving profits or by decreasing the number of people employed. In the modern business environment it is not possible for such a situation to continue unchanged.

Average wage per employee

Once again the importance of this ratio concerns competitiveness. If a company pays below the normal market rate for its people, it will tend in the long term to have a poorer quality workforce by failing to attract the best in the market, or retain its own best people.

Make sure that you are comparing like with like. If, for example, you compare two companies in the same business where one has the grand majority of its people in the UK and the other has a large number of staff in south-east Asia, you may find that the wages per

Is this a smart challenge

To consolidate your learning in this area, would it be worthwhile to build an industry average? Take an industry in which you are interested and get the annual reports of at least four big players in it. Aggregate the raw data by adding each of the items for the four companies together. This gives you a homegrown industry average.

Alternatively you can look these averages up in the various reference books that carry out this job for all industry sectors.

employee figure is much higher in the former. This may not indicate a problem for either company since the latter is operating in an environment of, at least at the present time, much lower wages generally.

5 Monitoring the Present

Introduction: financial accounts and management accounts

In Chapters 3 and 4 we looked at how companies measure financial success. We introduced the profit and loss account and the balance sheet as the two major statements used by accountants.

Financial accounting is concerned with the production of accounts, particularly for shareholders. The Companies Act in the UK and its equivalent in the USA govern the format of these accounts. Management accounts, on the other hand, are prepared in order to assist the managers of the business. There is no standard format. Management accounts should be presented in the way that is most helpful in the particular circumstances of the company concerned. They should contain sufficient detail to permit close control of the business.

Management accounts, therefore, play a very different role to financial accounts, and the time difference is enormous. It may be too late for some critical measures in some environments if information takes more than a week to get to the manager concerned. Smart managers pay a lot of attention to the management accounting system. After all, it is how senior managers judge their performance.

> **Smart test 18**
>
> If your management reports inform you that an entire sales team is performing below target, which of these is more likely to be effective remedial action?
>
> - Insist that each person spends more time in front of customers.
>
> - Look at the sales collateral they have in terms of sales aids, cost–benefit models, etc., and try to improve the productivity of the current time they spend in front of customers.

Compusell Inc.

One of Compusell's focuses is the telecommunications industry. An important growth area in telecommunications is wholesaling. In this environment a wholesaler will offer to route a telephone operator's calls through their switches for a certain cost. This cost changes all the time. A wholesaler on the immensely important North Atlantic route between the USA and Europe may, for a limited period of time, offer to route calls for less than cost in an effort to boost market share.

The competition has to have an extraordinarily fast management accounting system, which tells them, literally from hour to hour, the cost of routing calls through their network. If they use out-of-date information they could be boosting sales swiftly and losing money even faster.

The point of management accounts is that they give the trends in a business, a rolling reading of what is going on in the business, and they highlight the first signs of trouble.

Which comes first, the budget or the reporting system? Most companies operate with a budgeting system that has evolved over years. In the next chapter we will explain how those budgets are set and how to avoid being outsmarted in this big company ritual which more or less places the goalposts that will be used to measure managers' success. But arguably the starting point for internal measurement is the reporting measures which you need to control your part of the business.

From strategy to management accounting

A company or a division or a team sets a strategy. This results in their knowing what they are going to sell into which markets. They also know what their competitive advantage is. The team then decides which of these product markets to emphasize, which to sustain and which to slowly, or quickly, withdraw from. This leads to an operating plan that contains the targets that they will endeavour to achieve, first of all at team level, and secondly at individual level. The first requirement of the management accounting system is to report on progress, within an appropriate timeframe, against these targets. Each team and member of a team must be told in time and accurately the progress they are making.

> Perhaps the best illustration of what makes a good management accounting system is to look at the opposite. This is called skittle alley management and uses the analogy of teams of players playing skittles organized by management. The team is aware that the skittles are at the end of the alley, but management have carefully installed a curtain in front of them.
>
> The team members bowl, managers look behind the curtain and tell them how many they missed. Ridiculous, of course, but management accounting systems that have evolved over long periods of time frequently have elements of skittle alley management in them.

But it is not as simple as it seems. Knowing what your financial results are is often a good guide to management action. If you know on what measure you are falling short, you should investigate the right place to take remedial action. But knowing from the financial statements could already be too late. Let's look at a physical example as an analogy.

> Glass bottles are fabricated in kilns or ovens. The bottles are sensitive to changes in a number of physical conditions within the kiln such as temperature and pressure. They then come through into the cold end of the process and cool before being stored for shipment. On average they stay in inventory for 25 days before being shipped to a customer. At this moment the management accounting system records it as a sale. Allow the end of the month to arrive, the reports to be written and circulated before the sales and production teams know what is going on. Returns of below-quality bottles take another month to get into the system.
>
> If something has gone wrong in the hot end of the process it would be madness to wait for the sales teams to be told they are selling less and the production team to be told that they had fewer quality bottles and more rejects. You need the information on what is happening long before that, the moment the bottles get into the cold end, or more likely you put testing equipment into the hot end so that you know what is going wrong immediately and can take action to correct the temperature or pressure.
>
> Once again, ridiculous if you look at it like that, but that is how a lot of management reporting systems actually work.

Before we start the process of describing the attributes of a good management accounting system, we have to point out a fundamental flaw in profit centre management that all too often occurs in real life. Profit centre management is surely a good idea. If all the teams and divisions in the company are measured against the amount of profit they are generating and they all meet their targets, then surely the whole business is performing to the best of its capabilities. Not if you look at it like Norman Smart.

Smart Autos

Norman Smart is the owner and manager of a garage. He is proud of the reputation it has established in the local community and knows that there is good growth available to him if he continues to give good customer satisfaction and make profits. His strategy has been to concentrate on new car sales supported by close attention to after-sales support.

His accountants have advised him that the business has developed to such an extent that he should restructure the company into divisions. In their opinion such a structure will be better able to support the strong growth for which he is striving. Smart likes the plan because it gives him a chance to encourage his managers, whom he regards as very good, to develop their business skills.

Accordingly from the new company year there will be three departments. Alison Andrews will manage the new car sales department, Bob Beaumont the used car sales department and Chris Cook will control the service department. All three are pleased with the opportunity to show their ability.

Each manager is to run their department as an independent business. They will have to bear their share of central overheads, and deal with each other at arm's length, i.e. as an internal customer or supplier. Finally, in the plan there will be a bonus for each manager calculated as a percentage of profit.

The charging of overheads will be logically in three parts. Firstly, any overhead incurred by a department will be allocated to it. Secondly, a group of expenses, like rent, rates, electricity and insurance, will be charged on the basis of floor area occupied by each department. Finally, the recovery of other overheads will be achieved by a charge of 3% on each department's total revenue.

Smart feels that if each department pursues profit maximization, then the profits for the whole company will, by definition, be maximized. He states to all and sundry that the objectives for the year are growth, improved profits and a continuation of the company's high reputation for fairness and quality.

Along comes a regular customer. We'll make it you so that you can feel the potential pain that the new system passes to its customers. You wish to buy a new Ford, list price £18,000, and trade in your old one which you bought second-hand from Smart Autos two years ago. Smart Autos have serviced the car since then and at the last service they revealed that there was a lot of work required on the gearbox within the next few months and the service manager estimated the cost at £1,000.

You have decided to return to Smart Autos, since despite the gearbox problem, you feel they have given good value for money. You hope also that they will not take the gearbox work into account when they offer the trade-in price of, you estimate, £7,000. You know that there will be some flexibility on list price and hope to get a deal for £9,400. However, bearing in mind the gearbox problem you realize that you may need to go to £9,800. That, you think, gives you a reasonable deal and must give the car company an equally reasonable profit.

Now look at the situation from the managers' point of view. Here is an extract from the profit and loss account budget for the company.

Smart Autos: extract of the budget for the year

	New cars	Used cars	Service	Total
External sales	850	560	90	1500
Internal sales	350		80	430
Total revenue	1200	560	170	1930

Cost of sales				
New cars	700			700
Trade-in	380	90		470
Used internal		350		350
Repairs/servicing		80		80
Direct wages			45	45
Direct materials			37	37
Gross profit	120	40	88	248
Salaries	35	22	15	72
Departmental overhead	10	8	27	45
Rent etc,	8	6	6	20
Apportioned overhead	36	17	5	58
Total overheads	89	53	53	195
Net profit	31	−13	35	53

Now, let's look what happens in the company. Chris Cook gives Bob Beaumont a quote of £1,000 for the gearbox, plus 25 hours at £40 per hour for preparing the car for resale. This quote is in line with the instruction to treat internal customers at "arm's length", or as a separate business. It gives Chris a profit, after the 3% levy of £540.

Bob knows that the used car will only sell for £6,800. Out of this must come 3% for overheads as well as Chris's £2,000. The most Bob can offer Alison for the trade-in, allowing for a modest £400 profit, is £4,200.

The news stuns Alison. Her profit on selling a car at full price is only 20% or £3,600. Out of this must come her 3% levy on both the new car and the internal sale. This means that the customer must pay more than £10,800 on top of the trade-in for her just to break even. To earn a profit will mean an even higher price.

When Alison fails to convince you to pay this price – it is, remember, £1,000 above your top whack – she tries to renegotiate down the line. All three managers co-operate to draw up an estimate for break even as follows. In order to arrive at this, each manager has to reveal their costs. If you want to check the calculations, start with the service department, then used cars and finally you will arrive at the figure Alison needs to sell the new car for, i.e. £16,909.

	New cars	Used cars	Service
External sales	16,909	6,800	1,443
Internal sales	5,153		
Total revenue	22,062	6,800	1,443
Cost of sales			
New cars	14,400		
Trade-in	7,000		
Used internal		5,153	
Repairs/servicing		1,443	
Direct wages and materials			1,400
Apportioned overhead	662	204	43
Net profit	0	0	0

Alison must therefore ask you for £9,909 so that all departments break even. You go elsewhere since they are still above your maximum.

Consider what Norman Smart has lost. Ignoring the internal charges, they could have achieved the following:

New car sale (net)		9,800
Used car sale		6,800
		16,600
New car costs	14,400	
Repair costs	1,400	
		15,800
Profit		£800

Smart test 19

If an internal IT department charges telephone calls out to its internal customers at the cost to them plus 2% and their contribution to overheads is 8% of revenues, do they make more profit if their customers make more phone calls?

What are the attributes of a good management accounting system?

Right, now let's look at this thing positively and consider the nine attributes of a good management accounting system.

Attribute 1

A good system is produced as the result of frequent and effective communication between the accountants and the management of the business

It is a flaw in many teams' planning process to bring the accountants into the plan too late. No finance department can react immediately

A telephone company

Some of the call operators in a telephone company's call centres went on strike. The computerized management reporting system very accurately recorded the drop in productivity and the changes in calls answered, the time taken to pass people calling in from one person to another, etc., during the period of the strike. It did this extremely accurately by region, area and individual operator as well as nationally. The customers, working on a different set of success criteria, didn't notice any difference and were unaware when things had returned to normal.

> It takes the accountants a long time to work out a company's financial performance over any period. Annual reports are rarely published less than three months after the end of the year they cover. In a fast-moving environment, and given the creative accounting discussed in the previous chapter, a smart voice says, "By the time you interpret the report, you suddenly understand that the situation was irrecoverable eighteen months ago and that the company went bust last year."

to any single team's requirement for a different set of reporting information. Bring them in early and keep them involved.

Attribute 2

The system should not deal solely with the financial effects of what is happening. As we saw in the bottle-maker example, financial figures are what are known as lagging indicators. They tell what has gone wrong after the event. You need information that tells what is going wrong before it has a negative influence on the figures. The way to find what information you require is to ask the question "What factors are critical to my success?"

HAR Plc

It has been said that the reputation of a recruitment agency is only as good as the last recruit it placed. This is certainly true for repeat custom. You build a reputation by putting in people who live up to the opinion you gave of them and stay in the job for which they were recruited until the time comes for them to be internally promoted.

The opposite of this occurs when a customer comes back after three months looking for another person to replace a recruit who has been found to be not up to the job. How often will a customer keep faith with HAR? They know that with the best will in the world no recruiting agency is going to get it right every time, but lack of success cannot go on for ever.

Andy knows this and decides that the management accounting system must count the number of times a placement is unsuccessful for each customer. This has three benefits. It enables him to look into his executives who are having problems in this area, take proactive action when he feels that a customer is having a particularly bad time, and ensures that his executives follow up on all recruits since that is the only way they will collect that information.

Critical success factors are frequently concerned with activity rather than financial results. It is probably useful to distinguish activity from productivity although the two are intertwined. Productivity compares the financial revenue with the cost of the resources involved. Activity reports the raw data on the number of times something has occurred. It is worth remembering that activity reporting tends to be a much more sensitive issue with staff. They may be happy to have management comparing the number of people involved in achieving a target but less happy at having a count made of the number of times people stop work for ten minutes or the number of times they go to the loo. This "big brother" point is becoming more important as computers are used more and more in accurate and detailed activity reporting. You need to achieve the activity reporting objective without causing half your operators to stop cooperating or go on strike (see the example of the telephone company above).

HAR Plc

We have already seen how quickly a slow down in the economic cycle hits the order book and sales at HAR. One of the reasons that things got so far out of control was that middle management did not detect the slow down through the management accounting system.

They found out, obviously, when the monthly figures showed that fees for placements had declined. But this is two months after activity weakened.

The sales forecasting system did not help either. Their recruitment executives will not change their forecasts until they are absolutely sure that they are going to miss out on their numbers. No one likes predicting failure, and it is human nature to think that you can recover a situation from, say, a poor month. The trouble only becomes significant when all the executives are having the same problem – the signal of a change in the business environment.

What they needed was something in the management accounting system that accumulated the evidence of all the individual executives. They needed some sort of activity-monitoring system which measured how busy their agents were. Perhaps they should record the number of interviews being carried out, or even the number of telephone calls being made. This gives management more warning that something is up, and they can put into place some action to alleviate the situation.

> Can you control your business by the use of five or fewer measures that cover all your critical success factors?

Critical success factors are different for every business or department within a business. But you do need to identify them and resist the temptation to say that they cannot be measured. It is critical to the success of a copywriter that they write 2,000 words every day – easy to count. It is critical to the success of a restaurant that the toilets are inviting and clean. One of the ways you can measure that factor is by activity reporting.

Attribute 3

Management accounts must have credibility with managers so that

> **Accounting for every penny**
>
> It is a fact that every penny being spent by a company is the responsibility of an individual manager. Cross-charging should allocate the spend to the appropriate person. If cross-charging between departments happens haphazardly and has many errors or omissions, then management will disregard the accounting figures and ignore the underlying signals which the system should be sending. They then have the perfect excuse.
>
> The alternative to ignoring figures which do not reflect real life is for managers to spend hours arguing their case with the financial controllers to try and put the numbers right. This is also not good for business.

they take them seriously. It is a fact of business life that if any measures are less than totally rigorous, someone will use them to the disadvantage of the organization.

> **Smart test 20**
>
> If the accountants decide to change the depreciation policy of the fixed assets in your budget so that they are written off more quickly, what does this do to the return on assets target in your management report? How does it impact your cashflow?

How do you get to the stage where the management reports are accurate and reflect the real performance of teams in the field? Answer: with difficulty, particularly in big, diverse organizations with a multitude of disparate critical success factors.

So, both parties – the reporters and the reported on – need to do a deal whereby as well as senior managers striving to get a management accounting system which is suitable, at the end of the day managers must in their turn accept that their performance is going to be measured as it is reported in the management accounting system. It should be fair to both parties: the measured and the measurers.

> Would you be happy if someone from the planet Mars arrived and decided on your level of remuneration or bonus by looking coldly and dispassionately at your performance against your management accounts system?

Attribute 4

The management accounting system should concentrate on as small a number of key measures as possible, so that managers can control all of them at the same time. Most people keep the really important management control figures for their job in their heads. They roughly know before the reports come in how they are doing. The

> **Make sure you can control the controls**
>
> Managers in an accounting firm were judged on just four performance measures:
>
> - Work in progress, i.e. work that has been done for clients but not yet billed
>
> - Debtors, i.e. how long it took them to get their bills paid by clients
>
> - Recovery rates, i.e. the fee charged expressed as a percentage of the cost of the time put into the activity
>
> - Percentage of chargeable time, i.e. how many of the 240 working days per year, or 1,680 hours, were billable to clients
>
> The partners in the firm were soon found to be able to monitor only two of these at any one time. By the time they had looked at two measures for variances, differences between budget or target and actual, and talked to the accountants who were responsible for them, the next set of management accounts were coming out. The more streetwise of the accountants found out which measures were due to be flavour of each month and made absolutely certain that they were well within budget for those two in that month. They did this even at the expense of wide variances on the others. You could say that the partners were chasing them round the budgeting cycle and never catching them.
>
> Trying to control all four measures at the same time was like trying to squeeze a balloon – the air always escapes somewhere and causes a bulge.

art of management reporting is to capture these measures. There is also a limit to how many measures your boss can monitor, and you quickly know where an abundance of so-called controls have left loopholes through which the smart manager can drive a coach and horses.

What you have to avoid is this. Don't let middle managers keep senior managers in the dark because of a blame culture. In a blame culture a manager is in less trouble if everything appears to be going well even if it is not (answer: change the culture); or middle managers are economical with the truth because of the bonus scheme (answer: change the incentives because they are doing more harm than good).

> On the one hand:
>
> - If you are paid bonuses to hit certain measures, are you aware enough of the incentive scheme and the accounting systems that support it so that you can maximize the return on your performance?
>
> On the other hand:
>
> - If you pay bonuses to people, how confident are you that the incentives really reward performance that works in favour of the overall business performance and strategy? Remember Smart Autos.

Attribute 5

A good management accounting system gives clear indications to managers and avoids delivering impenetrable lists of irrelevant numbers. Managers should only receive the data that they need to run their part of the organization. Sometimes managers spend a lot of time picking out the information they require from the load of information sent to them on a regular basis.

Compusell Inc.

It is quite possible to disseminate information too widely. When Sally first went into sales she found that all the salespeople in the team were given information about each other's performance and about the performance of their manager. This was fine in good times when they were all jockeying for the position of "Who is farthest over target this month?" It was not so great when times were hard and people were taking different amounts of time to adapt to the new situation. There was a growing morale problem until management limited reports to what the individual required.

Attribute 6

A good system must assist in detecting the secondary effect of some trends in the numbers. Sometimes numbers, which are looking good, are actually concealing a problem.

Compusell Inc.

Another good example from Compusell is the way that the numbers are related to each other. For example, it is often true that an improvement in cashflow and revenues can mask a problem with the order book unless all three are reported on and linked in some way.

Attribute 7

The accounting system needs to show comparisons and trends as well as the absolute numbers. This is more difficult in a seasonal business when the real comparison that managers need is what is happening this year with what happened last year, rather than the simpler thing to report last month against this.

Compusell Inc.

Here is Sally's profit and loss account. This is the information that forms the basis of her control over the team's performance.

Previous year	This year	Budget	Year end forecast
Quarters 1–3	Quarters 1–3	Quarters 1–3	*

*For each item this column will be marked red, amber or green. The system will have preset levels when the three indicators will be triggered. Red will indicate that urgent action is probably required. Amber will show when something is moving out of line. Green items probably need no attention.

Sales This records the total of the list price of revenues. Since there is a comparison between the same period last year as this, any seasonal issues are looked after. A percentage column gives a quick indicator of comparative progress.

Discounts These are the amounts deducted from list price. Notice how at this level there is no distinction between products. You may need more detailed information to isolate product problem areas eg where there is competitive price pressure.

Net sales This is the total of invoices sent out.

Cost of goods sold Different companies calculate this in different ways. It is necessary to find out how this is done to make sure that it is relevant and a fair measure.

Manufacturing general Contribution to manufacturing overheads measured in some way related to the cost of goods sold.

Software levy Contribution to the software development fund. A device to make sure that everyone is making a contribution to new software being written now.

Sales expenses The cost of the selling team responsible for this profit and loss account. The amount of control the manager has over this is limited. It is likely that salaries and other people related expenses will eat up 80% of it. The team leaders have little control over people expenses. If they economize on people they are bound to lose sales.

Administration Some of this may be direct costs of the people Sally has doing the administration in her team. The rest will be her portion of the general overheads.

Depreciation Sally owns her own assets and the depreciation is a charge against her.

Earnings from operations This is probably the main profit measure at Sally's level.

Nominal cost of capital Most management accounts have some cost allocated for the cost of capital. It may be interest charged which is worked out by the bottom line cashflow of this report. In Compusell, which borrows no money, it has developed a nominal cost of capital. This is calculated from the return on capital the company requires its operations to make. We will look at this in greater detail in Chapter 7.

Profit before taxes The profit figure after deducting the cost of capital.

Taxes There will be a 'marginal rate' of tax which Compusell levies on its operations. It is basically the top rate of tax which the company pays, or an agreed average.

Net profit/loss after taxes The bottom line.

Cashflow All the above items are cash items except depreciation and the software levy which is an internal charge. The cashflow therefore will add these back. Once again more of this in Chapter 7.

Attribute 8

A good management reporting system avoids misleading managers into making poor decisions. To start understanding the positive attributes of management accounting systems that assist decision making, we will go back to one view of cost allocation which does indeed mislead decision makers.

Management accounting starts from what we have already studied, of which the following can be used as a template:

	No. of units	Price per unit	Total
Sales			
Direct costs			
Materials			
Labour			
Overhead costs			
Administration			
Selling			
Profit			

Such a view of the world of internal finance offers, however, many problems and anomalies. Suppose a company sells only one product and sells it for £400. Its business plan this year is to sell 1,000 units at a profit of £40 each. Their budgeted profit and loss account looks like this.

	No. of units	Price per unit	Total
Sales	1,000	400	400,000
Direct costs			
Materials	1,000	150	150,000
Labour	1,000	90	90,000
Total direct costs		240	240,000
Overhead costs			
Administration		80	80,000
Selling		40	40,000
Total cost		360	360,000
Profit		40	40,000

They have a big export opportunity. An agent has come to them and said that he has a client who wants to purchase 200 units but that the price must not exceed £320. At first glance this seems impossible, since the total cost per unit is, at £360, higher than the offered sales price. Such a transaction would reduce profits. Or would it?

The agent has come to the company, so there are no real selling costs. Similarly the administration department as it is can cope with the billing and other administration without incurring extra cost. This means that we could revise the profit and loss account to look like this.

	No. of units	Price per unit	Total
Sales	1,000	400	400,000
	200	320	64,000
Total sales	1,200		464,000
Direct costs			
Materials	1,200	150	180,000
Labour	1,200	90	108,000
		240	288,000
Overhead costs			
Administration		80,000	
Selling		40,000	
Total cost		408,000	
Profit		56,000	

In absolute terms we can see that profits have gone from £40,000 to £56,000. But redoing the profit and loss account for each such incident is cumbersome, and it does not help us to know some key information such as "What is the lowest price we could sell this product for and still make additional profits?" Attribute 9 solves this.

Attribute 9

A good management accounting system assists managers to make good decisions based upon the real situation rather than a theoretical or notional view of the costs of the business. Some people call it the contribution method of allocating costs.

We can solve the dilemma posed above and make management accounting systems useful and flexible if we classify costs in the operation into fixed and variable costs.

- Fixed costs are those that do not change with an increase in volume of sales. You do not need to pay for more board members if the salesforce brings in more orders. Similarly there are no further costs in administration and so on. In the example above the fixed costs are deemed to be the administration and selling lines.

- Variable costs are those that do vary with volume of sales. For the purpose of this exercise we will regard the material and labour costs as variable.

In fact real life is not as simple as this. While materials probably do vary in direct proportion to number of units produced, labour probably does not.

The original way of breaking down a unit selling price was into vari-

Creative accounting

An interesting paradox arises from this classification. When the final profit and loss account for a period is drawn up, variable costs will appear to be fixed per unit sold, while fixed costs, of course, are fixed overall but vary per unit, since they are divided among the number of units sold.

In this way it is possible to find an answer to the question, "How can we improve our profits without selling more units or reducing our fixed or variable costs?" The answer is to make more units even though you do not sell them.

What happens is that you build up inventory. The value of each unit that goes into inventory is its variable cost plus its share of the fixed costs. You do not account for the expenses of the unit until you sell it. So profits have gone up because the fixed costs have been divided into more units.

So, the next time you see a car manufacturer whose chairman's statement includes the words "We increased our profits this year despite a difficult year for sales of new vehicles", check how many new vehicles are parked on the factory forecourt.

able costs per unit, fixed costs per unit and profit per unit. The contribution approach splits the selling price into only two components – variable costs and contribution calculated as the selling price minus the variable costs.

Before looking at how the contribution method can be used in decision making, let us for a moment consider whether such accurate calculation of the financial aspects of the business of making products and selling them is worthwhile. Let us consider HAR and Compusell, making slight adjustments to their sales plans, and look at the financial result.

HAR and Compusell

Sally Cranfield of Compusell and Andy McRae at HAR have very different problems. Sally has to increase sales of computer products and services to her accounts. She has to do it profitably but the important measures are orders and deliveries or revenue. This is made more significant by the fact that the salespeople under her are targeted solely on orders. This brings her under huge pressure to make each proposal as competitive as possible, particularly in terms of price.

Here is the estimated profit and loss account for a deal in which her people are involved.

	No. of units	Price per unit	Total
Sales	100	10	1,000
Variable costs	100	6	600
Fixed costs			300
Profit			100

The salesperson involved in the sale gives her one problem, production give her another and administration a third. The customer, she is informed by the salesperson, wants to buy from Compusell, but has had a cheaper offer. He thinks that if Sally could knock just 2% off the price per unit, he can take a case for buying from Compusell to his board. That discount plus reducing the order to only 98 units will make his budget work.

Production have had the agreement of management to a slight increase in the price of the unit, it's only 2%, but in the circumstances she cannot pass this on to the customer.

Administration has been saying for some time that there would be a slight increase in their costs due to increased charges from the IT department. It's only 2%

Sally recalculates the profit and loss account for this project and finds the following.

	No. of units	Price per unit	Total
Sales	98	9.80	960.40
Variable costs	98	6.12	599.76
Fixed costs			306
Profit		54.64	

Each 2% adjustment, all to Sally's disadvantage, has combined to knock nearly 46% off the profit of this deal.

Over at HAR Andy is also taking a number of seemingly small decisions aimed at starting the process of re-establishing profitability. His executives sell a package of material to clients which keeps them up to date on matters to do with employment law.

A major HAR client is likely to buy 100 of these and Andy wonders if the executive could do better. "I want every one to sell just a few more of these", he says to the executives, "Get each client to take just 2% more copies even though we are increasing the selling price a little, by 2%."

He buys the package from a printer/packager whom he convinces should lower the cost to HAR just a fraction, just 2%.

He had also been working for a while on the administration function and told them to find some economies, "Every little helps", he says, "Just knock me 2% off what you spend right now.

Andy's starting point was exactly the same as Sally's but he has made the slight adjustments in his favour.

The deal to the major client now looks like this:

	No. of units	Price per unit	Total
Sales	102	10.20	1,040.40
Variable costs	102	5.88	599.76
Fixed costs			294
Profit			146.64

When the 2% works for us the addition to the profit is over 46%. If you think of Compusell doing similar deals all over the world you can see the huge difference it could make. Andy also thinks about this in wider terms and tries to get a culture going in the company where everyone is looking for ways to improve profits by small adjustments rather than huge upheaval. It may not be enough, but it's a start.

Responsibility accounting

So, it is worthwhile getting down to the detail, but we have to avoid the Smart Autos débâcle. How do we do it? The answer lies in responsibility accounting. You need to organize your management accounting system so that managers can truly control their profitability, make their contribution to overheads over which they have control, but not laden them with overheads out of their reach. It might look like this:

	Divisional management accounts	Note	Products A B C	Total
	Sales	1		
Minus	Variable costs	2		
	= Contribution	3		
Minus	Fixed costs controlled by division	4		
	= Contribution controllable by manager of division	5		
Minus	Fixed costs incurred by division but controlled by head office	6		

	= Divisional contribution to head office costs	7
Minus	Apportionment of head office costs 8	8
	Divisional profit	9

The columns for products provide this information by product line or type of service as far down as the line for contribution.

Notes

1 These are the division's sales recorded by product.

2 These are the variable costs of producing the products sold.

3 We call sales minus variable costs the contribution. This gives a measure of the relative profitability of each product.

4 The fixed costs over which the divisional manager has complete control.

5 Controllable contribution. This is a fair measure of the success of the divisional manger and we can use it for evaluation purposes. The division's managers will use it to get a proper estimate of implementing new ideas or reacting to an unexpected opportunity. Such decisions are not affected by similar decisions being made in other divisions, and we have avoided the Smart Autos syndrome.

6 An example of this might be the IT costs incurred if head office gives the division no right to go elsewhere for this service. The same could go for transport or facilities. Similarly if head office controls the decision over investment in fixed assets for the division, then the depreciation figure will appear here.

7 This contribution is a good indicator of the short-term viability or success of the division. We can look at making more costs controllable by the division or remain convinced that head office should remain in charge of these costs. At least we can see them.

8 There are some costs that are not incurred by the division but have to be paid for. In here we would find the costs of the board itself and possibly the human resources department. The term apportionment indicates a recharge on a fair but arbitrary basis – possibly based on sales turnover.

9 This bottom line gives us a fair measure of the long-term viability or potential of the division.

But it can still go badly wrong. Head office must allow that their costs, which are apportioned to the divisions, must make some sort of contribution or be cut. Here is what happens if the head office believes that its costs are inevitable and fixed.

When it all goes horribly wrong

In this case head office costs of £24 million are allocated to divisions by turnover.

Division	A	B	C	Total
Turnover	100	50	50	200
Divisional contribution	18	7	5	30
Head office costs	12	6	6	24
Profit	6	1	(1)	6

The long-term viability of division C is plainly not there and the decision is taken regretfully to close the division. By definition, head office costs are unaffected in total and need to be reallocated.

Division	A	B	Total
Turnover	100	50	150
Divisional contribution	18	7	25
Head office costs	16	8	24
Profit	2	(1)	1

Oh dear, now Division B faces the chop.

Division	A	Total
Turnover	100	100
Divisional contribution	18	18
Head office costs	24	24
Profit	(6)	(6)

Neat, eh? By refusing to believe that head office costs were not directly linked to the contribution of the divisions, we are forced, once again with great regret, logically to close the business. A silly example but you can see the point.

Operating leverage

A last point on the use of management accounts in decision making. There is a huge benefit to be gained if a division or a company can increase its sales volumes without increasing its fixed costs. It illustrates what managers are often talking about: "We have to sweat the assets." When you have spent money on infrastructure of any sort, slight increases in sales have an unexpectedly high impact on the bottom line. The concept of operating leverage shows the benefit of this.

As always, the upside potential of leverage is matched by the downside risk. If you have operating leverage of 5, then a 10% improvement in your sales will produce a 50% improvement in you profits. A 10% drop in sales will produce 5 times that decrease in profits.

The impact of leverage has another dimension when you look at in terms of dependency on customers. It is quite possible to lose an important customer. Suppose your biggest customer does 20% of

Operating leverage

Look at the impact on the bottom line of different splits between variable and fixed costs. Each of the four profit and loss accounts is built to answer the same question. "If we can increase sales volume by 10% without increasing fixed costs, what percentage impact will it have on net profit?" Operating leverage is calculated by dividing this percentage by 10%.

First case

	£ Current	£ Additional 10%
Sales	100	110
Variable costs	90	99
Contribution	10	11
Fixed costs	0	0
Net profit	10	11 (an increase of 10%)

The operating leverage is 1, i.e. there is no leverage at all.

Second case

	£ Current	£ Additional 10%
Sales	100	110
Variable costs	60	66
Contribution	40	44
Fixed costs	30	30
Net profit	10	14 (an increase of 40%)

The operating leverage is 4.

Third case

	£ Current	£ Additional 10%
Sales	100	110
Variable costs	30	33
Contribution	70	77
Fixed costs	60	60
Net profit	10	17 (an increase of 70%)

The operating leverage is 7.

Fourth case

	£ Current	£ Additional 10%
Sales	100	110
Variable costs	0	0
Contribution	100	110
Fixed costs	90	90
Net profit	10	20 (an increase of 100%)

The operating leverage is 10.

your business, but because of operating leverage losing that sales turnover would wipe out your entire profit. It can easily be the case.

HAR and Compusell

A State Department client of Sally's has $1 million left in their IT budget towards the end of their financial year. They ask Sally to make a proposal to supply goods and services to this amount for, obviously, projects which will bring benefits to the organization.

Sally and her account manager have a number of plans for the account, most of which involve selling equipment that has a variable cost of 75%. Another plan involves selling consultancy services. She has the consultants already on board, so the leverage of selling them is very high. She chooses to sell the consultancy service because the sales value comes straight through to the bottom line.

It is because HAR's cost structure is mainly fixed that they find it difficult to reduce costs when sales fall. That is, in the terminology here, their operating leverage is high. As a defensive measure, Andy needs to arrange for some of the fixed costs to be replaced by variable costs. There are various methods of doing this include outsourcing and persuading staff to accept a different remuneration system. We will see him do this in Chapter 8.

> **Smart test 21**
>
> Assume that your operating profit is £500,000 and your operating leverage is 6.75. If sales decline by 10%, by how much does your profit go down?

Converting the profit and loss into cashflow

Why we have to do it

As we have said, it is possible for a company to be showing profits in the accounts but be failing for lack of cash. The major reason for this is that the profit and loss account will show the cost of fixed assets being spread over a long period, whereas the cash payment needs to be made at once.

For this reason companies will always look at cashflow forecasts as well as the budgeted profit and loss accounts when considering future company performance.

Typically a company will prepare a budgeted profit and loss account first and then convert this into a cashflow forecast by adjusting for timing of payments. We will make more use of the concept of cashflow in Chapter 7.

> **Kaplan and Norton**
>
> These two smart voices advocate the concept in management accounting of the balanced scorecard. This requires the system to give information in four different areas:
>
> Customers   This answers the question "How do they see us?"
>
> Internal   "What must we excel at?"
>
> Financial   "How do shareholders see us?"
>
> Innovation "How can we continue to learn, improve and add value?"

Work to a balanced score card

Before we leave the topic of management accounting systems we must emphasize that many companies are looking at themselves in a more comprehensive way than simply at their figures. Shareholders also are thinking about business more holistically, taking a broader look at an organization's activities to assess its long-term future.

The key idea of the balanced scorecard is that a business, and therefore its managers, has a responsibility for more than just *profits*. Here is another expression of the same concept.

Managers are also responsible for the level of *customer service* they offer. This is true whether the customers are external in terms of people who pay cash for products and services or internal where a service is provided within the business by, for example, the IT department to the rest of the business.

They also have to meet a series of *quality* targets concerned with reliability, competitiveness and innovation.

Finally they have to operate with some form of *environment* targets. All companies are required to work within legal environmental constraints; many are keeping a step ahead of the regulations and doing their bit for the planet.

The headings in each topic could be as follows, and management may care to set operating targets as well as strategic targets for each of them.

Profits	**Customer service**
Measured by:	Measured by:
Division	Delivery dates
Product	Complaints
Service	Business processes
Market region	Activity levels
Age of product	Time to repair
Bought in/built here	Mean time between failures

Quality
Measured by:
   Strategic innovation
   Product innovation
   Competitiveness
   Returns
   Warranty repairs
   Reliability

Environment
Measured by:
   Raw materials used
   Packaging type and amount
   Supplier compliance
   Energy used
   Waste and recycling
   Pollution

There are as many ways to present management accounts as there are companies. It is advisable occasionally to take a step back and reconsider whether your current way of reporting is still the best way. But this book is about business finance, so let's get back to matters to do with money.

6 Planning for the Future

Setting budgets which make sense

What is a budget?

Smart managers deliver on time and within budget. If you can just do that, you will already have put yourself into the top few per cent of managers. Most people fail on this simple rule time after time. So, let's look at the topic of budgeting. A budget is simply a plan. Strictly, a budget is a plan expressed in financial terms but companies will, for example, produce budgets for material usage, manpower requirements and other resources as well as for accounting purposes. Indeed, we will see that budgets which overemphasize the financial side can give much less help to the managers of the business.

As we turn our attention from the measurement of past performance to planning for and predicting the future, we will always be using management accounts. This is because accurate budgeting will require detailed information of costs and revenues. The budgeting system or cycle tends to be an annual ritual. Divisions and departments are required to make detailed estimates of what they expect to earn and spend for the next year. Such a narrow, time-dependent focus can lead to horrible anomalies.

Surviving the budgeting battle

Managers are frequently forced into seeing the budgeting round as a battle. We use the term advisedly since the tactics of the people involved obey more of the law of the jungle than the laws of economic good management. They are being asked to predict what is going to happen one year ahead, knowing that they will be held responsible for variances to the budget if they get it wrong. And being normal human beings, they do not want to have, or be perceived as having, a lesser job than they had last year.

So much for the owners of the budget. They also have a boss who is looking at the battle from his or her point of view. People who agree budgets with subordinates are keen to be seen by their superiors as taking no nonsense from their people and setting challenging earnings budgets and miserly expenditure budgets.

Here is what to do to protect yourself and your dug out:

- Inflate your budget by 10% on the grounds that after a long series of negotiations your boss will pull it back by that amount. This makes everybody happy, you have got the budget you first thought of and your boss can report a hard battle well won.

- Never reveal that there is slack in the budget. If there is one corner of the budget that is set traditionally but does not need to be spent, keep mum. You will have a little pot of gold to put into areas where you actually need to spend money. This is a whole lot easier in the heat of battle than persuading your superiors that there is a real case for increased spending.

- Spend it or lose it. This is a particularly irrational battleground in the war at government department level. If you fail to spend money budgeted for this year, then next year's budget will be cut by that amount. This leads to remarkable amounts of energy going into chasing suppliers to deliver, on the one hand, and getting the invoice through the system, on the other, during the last week of the year.

- If you have left it until the last minute: take last year's budget, add inflation, 10% for negotiating slack, see above, and keep the item description as vague as possible. That way you will probably be able to twist and turn during the year to come and come in on target.

All of these tips have nothing really to do with the success of the venture but are reasonable survival techniques. If your boss complains, tell him or her that nobody said life was fair either.

Why is it right to set a budget three months before the start of the company year every year? This question is particularly appropriate if you work in a fast-moving industry where change occurs frequently and product lifecycles are short. For the sake of realism and practicality we are going to discuss how this annual ritual takes place, but before that let us start at a more logical point: the overall strategy.

Compusell Inc.

At a suitable moment in the company year, Sally reviews the team's strategy. One of the end products of this strategy will be an overall outline budget that she will then be able to turn into the detailed company figures required by the budgeting system.

She bases her budget on the product market emphasis she and the team will place over the next sensible period of planning time – say two years. Notice how she talks of product markets. The argument goes that nothing is a product unless it has a market, and a market is irrelevant unless you are considering selling a product into it.

This leads her to draw up a product market matrix with the products down the left-hand side and the markets across the top. The team can examine each cell in this matrix, decide on the current focus – low, medium or high – and discuss and decide on the focus for the period of the strategy. They can then estimate their earnings stream for each product market.

They look at their costs very logically, using not the company's detailed forms but a simple expenditure list

- Inputs (materials, information and services)
- Facilities
- Equipment
- People
- Cash (since they are charged for the use of the company's money)

Subtract the expenditure from the earnings and Sally has a first stab at her profit aspiration that may drive her back to re-examine some of the product market emphasis.

This gives the team an outline budget figure that reflects their strategy, and is a much better starting point for budgeting than getting out last year's numbers. They still have much to do to get it into the form required for budgets and to make business cases (see next chapter for capital expenditure).

There can be a difficult divide in this area between finance people and the manager of the business. Finance people cannot understand what the problem is: "Take last year's budget figures, all it is is a list of figures, and project it forward into next year." But, as Sally's case shows, a change in strategy may very well change how the budget figures should be made up. Suppose the new strategy is for virtual teams to be set up by project. The old budget did not allow for such a grouping of resources. It had it only by function and grades. So unless they talk, Sally and the accountants are going to have two separate views of the budget, and Sally will have to do her own calculations to find out how the virtual teams are performing. She wants to start with a clean sheet, which the accountants might call zero-based budgeting.

Budgets should achieve three objectives:

1 They should assist in the planning process of the company.

2 They should help in co-ordinating the activities of the various parts of the organization.

3 They should enable the company to control its operations.

In addition, the budgetary *process* should be useful in forcing management to examine closely the operations of the company so as to produce a viable budget.

How companies set budgets

The starting point will always be the sales budget. It is the sales budget that determines the level of materials and staff required, the production budget and machinery usage. From the sales budget we can determine costs and hence profit.

So how is a sales budget set? Three factors will be taken into account:

- What is our past experience? What trends can we identify which may help us predict sales this year?

- What is the current state of the market? What do the sales director and staff say about current prospects?

- What sales level would be required to achieve the profit target set by the directors?

HAR plc

Andy has divided the way forward into two parts: the short term, by which he means the next six months, and the longer term. From his cashflows he knows that he will need external finance for both of these. He needs to persuade his bankers in the short term not to continue to require him to repay short-term debt, and to increase the short-term facility available to him. He knows that the starting point of both of these is to have a series of budgets which are credible in the first place and which he can deliver on. You can always borrow money if the lender believes that you are going in the future to be in a position to pay the interest and repay the loan. Andy needs this credibility badly. He starts from the six-month sales forecast and asks his executives to make their estimates as realistic as they can. He persuades them not to put down the figures that they think he and the bankers would like to see, but to make an honest and real attempt to forecast the future.

He gets them to divide the prospects into four categories:

- Category A: those orders that are already in.
- Category B: those orders that have been agreed by the customer but for which contracts have not been signed or purchase orders raised. Probably three out of four of these will become orders.

- Category C: good prospects that have a good chance of at least half being converted into sales.
- Category D: prospects that can be identified as particular opportunities but which have some way to go before they can be thought to be likely to happen. Say one in four of these will convert.

Andy then treats each category as follows to get to his best shot at a forecast: 100% of category A total plus 75% of B plus 50% of C plus 25% of D. While he cannot be sure exactly where the sales revenue will come from, he should have the total sales more or less right.

With three months' practice and experience the executives become skilled in their sales predictions and the bank starts to have some faith in HAR's ability to achieve its sales budget. This may still be well below what is required to reestablish profitability but that, at this stage, was not the objective.

Any budget produced from these factors must then be tested for feasibility by reference to production capacity, staff availability and other constraints on delivering products or services.

Smart test 22

If you give bonuses as a sales incentive, is it wise to put a cap on what the salespeople can earn by setting a top limit for bonuses?

Budgets may not always be a prediction of what management consider will happen. Management often use them as a means of motivating staff to achieve better performance. In this case, the budget will be set at a level higher than it is expected will actually be achieved. In striving to reach the budget, staff will improve their performance.

The danger with this is that, if the budget is set too high, then staff will be demotivated because they see the budget as unattainable. But the budget is a way for senior managers to pass down to their people the facts of business life. There was a good example of this in Compusell. In any case, setting budgets too low encourages staff to relax their efforts back to meet the budget. Slack is built in to future budgets and the problem gets worse.

To deal with this, management may sometimes set a "public" budget for use by staff, while retaining their own private budget showing what they really expect to happen.

From the sales budget we can prepare the following budgets:

- Production budget

- Manufacturing budget, subdivided into materials budget, labour budget and manufacturing overheads budget

- Administration costs (indirects) budget

- Selling and distribution costs budget

- Capital expenditure budget

Compusell Inc.

In the early days of personal computers the PC division of Compusell realized a horrible truth. If they did not follow the market in reducing prices they would not sell PC's in significant numbers. If they grew sales by even 25%, which is pretty high growth, at that competitive price, then the division would not even cover its cost of production. The only way the figures would work was to demand a doubling of sales and production.

They set this as a budget. All the salespeople's targets were lifted 100% from last year. You can imagine their reaction. However, the marketing department as well as the finance department were doing their jobs well. The market did offer such growth, the salespeople achieved their targets and Compusell stayed in the PC business.

All of these budgets start from the increased figure for sales and will call widely on last year's budget in setting the new one. These may then be combined to give a budgeted profit and loss account, a cash budget and a budgeted balance sheet for the organization.

Typically, the budgets building into the profit and loss account will be prepared for a year and analysed into quarterly or monthly periods. Some companies constantly update their budgets to plan 12 months ahead (a rolling budget). It is more common, however, as we have seen, to plan once a year for the following financial year.

It is particularly important that the cash budget is prepared on a monthly basis so that managers can monitor it regularly. The capital expenditure budget is different. It will need to consider cashflows throughout the life of proposed projects and therefore may stretch for many years. It is unusual to go into too much detail about the timing of cashflows in a capital budget. Such timings are in any case difficult to predict. It is probably as well for the company to concern itself with the net cashflow arising each year as a result of capital spending projects. We will deal with this in depth in the next chapter.

HAR plc

In fact, at this stage in the survival process Andy is looking at his cash forecast on a daily basis, deciding what and whom he can pay. He keeps suppliers well informed of progress. They want their money if it is owed, but are likely to prefer to get it late than not at all.

Practical problems with budgeting

1. Predicting demand

Part of the solution to this is to use activity levels to iron out bias Companies usually try to break down their sales into product lines and sales areas and predict demand for each individually. Hopefully, this will result in the under- and overestimates balancing out in the total budget. Further, control will be made easier when the company identifies a shortfall later on.

Compusell Inc.

Salespeople and sales managers have a bias in the way they forecast their likely sales. Some will show very high figures. The type of person who forecasts too high is often one who wants to report to managers what they believe the managers want to hear. It is a skill of sales management to detect this and scale down.

On the other hand, there are those sales people who constantly understate their forecast. Their reason is, perhaps, that they are trying to show how difficult is the task which they have been allocated. In such cases the manager has to scale up.

Since it is the starting point for the other budgets, an inaccurate sales forecast drives poor production plans and can potentially cost a lot of money. In Compusell they have tackled this problem with activity monitoring in the management accounting system which counts the number of quotations sent out during the accounting period as well as the actual orders taken. In this case the system is genuinely helping to iron out the inaccuracies of such subjective reports as the sales forecast.

It is possible to use statistical techniques for forecasting demand but it is doubtful whether these are actually much more reliable than simply relying on experience. Having said that, you will probably need some process for calculating total sales from chance factors. Here is an example from HAR.

HAR plc

The major accounts sales manager for HAR has a quarterly forecasting problem. He is responsible for looking after the ten biggest accounts which HAR has and which produce some 45% of total sales revenues.

One of his customers is predicting an expansion of 50 people, all of whom, in theory, could be found and placed by HAR. They have agreed terms and conditions that guarantee no competition to HAR for the next year, but there is some doubt over the timing of the expansion. If all goes well it could all happen in this quarter, but delay could take some or all of them into the next quarter or even the one after. The sales manager uses his experience and a conversation with the customer to give the project a fifty–fifty chance of happening this quarter. This results in 25 placements as the forecast for this client.

Another client is busy recruiting at least 40 people. They are using a number of agencies and encouraging HAR and others to compete to put up the best candidates. The sales manager knows that there is no chance of HAR finding all 40, and feels that getting a quarter of them would be a reasonable performance. He forecasts forty at 25% – ten people.

In this way the quarterly forecast builds. Probably none of the figures forecast will be exactly right, but this weighting by chance factors gives an estimate which in the overall will be satisfactorily accurate.

To deal with the problem of uncertainty in sales, some companies produce a variety of predictions based on most likely, optimistic and pessimistic estimates of demand. This will highlight the effect on profit if sales are not at the desired level. An alternative approach is to perform a sensitivity analysis that asks what the effect on profit will be of changes in demand. We will deal with both of these techniques in the context of project evaluation or investment appraisal.

2. Predicting production costs

This should not present the same level of difficulty as sales since the relationship between production and the quantity of material and labour used will be well established.

There will be the problem of predicting the level of inflation to use but this should not introduce major problems into a single year budget. Inflation is more of a problem when dealing with long-term project evaluation.

So, there are some good reasons for asking people to keep to each element of the budget rather than just achieving the overall result. It is a question of getting the level of detail right.

3. Slack

Expense budgets are often based on previous year's figures. This has

> **Running a hotel down profitably**
>
> In a large hotel chain one manager has a terrific reputation for restoring budget profitability for hotels that are not on target. He was moved from hotel to hotel and each time a pattern emerged. He brought the hotel's profits back on track, moved on, and the next manager in had terrific difficulties maintaining the margins achieved.
>
> What the smart manager did was to kill all expenditure on maintenance and repairs. He put broken chairs in the cellar and covered over the cracks. This worked for the period of time he was there, but meant that the new manager coming in behind had to pick up the extra expenses for repairs that should have been done previously.

two effects. Firstly, it may not be necessary to repeat previous year's expenditure where this was of a one-off nature. This builds slack into the budget and hence control is lost. We have seen how a manger can use this to his or her advantage. Secondly, knowing that next year's budget will be based on this year's spend, the budget-holder makes sure to spend the whole budget this year even if it is not entirely necessary. Seen from the other point of view, slack makes the third objective of budgeting – keeping the business under control – difficult to achieve. The solution to this problem is to insist that the budget is detailed and all items justified each year.

Motivation

Staff often see budgets as a threat since, in the end, their superiors impose them. Even where the budget holder's input is sought at the planning stage, the final budget often bears little resemblance to the draft.

HAR plc

If you move costs from fixed into variable you reduce risk and decrease your margin. Andy uses this as another small adjustment to performance. Currently his executives have on-target earnings of £40,000, made up of £30,000 and 10% on sales. This means that achieving a £100,000 sales budget makes on target earnings. He offers to increase the rate of bonus and reduce their salaries. This means that on-target earnings will go up a bit, otherwise the executives will not accept the new scheme, but Andy's profits are less damaged if the executive fails to achieve budget.

He has moved some of the executive's earnings from fixed costs into variable. This is a good example of operating leverage, which we covered in Chapter 5.

There is no doubt that real participation in planning and budgeting will lead to a greater commitment from budget-holders and also better performance. Unfortunately this is another area where a company having difficulties is put at additional disadvantage. The fundamental truth is that if a business is doing well the people in control are the business managers who have the vision and knowledge to look for new opportunities. When a company is performing below its expectations, power will tend to move towards the people in control of the finances. This may not be good for business since their concentration will be on short-term survival and recovery.

> **Is this a smart challenge?**
>
> How seriously do you take your company's budgeting system? Would it be a good idea to go through a process of strategic planning to produce a real overall budget before you go into the standard budgeting cycle?

7 Never Mind the Profits, Feel the Cashflow

Introduction

You are now in a position where you can read a profit and loss account, examine an annual report, look at a set of management accounts, and not only understand them but comment on their quality. We have moved from historical records to the use of management accounts in making decisions for the future. What we now need to do is look further into the future. We need to get into a position where we can convert estimates for business success into a convincing story of why one project should be preferred against another. We said in the last chapter that smart managers deliver on time and within budget. They also weigh up in advance the return they are going to make from each decision they take.

Compusell Inc.

Sally is discussing with one of her account managers the possibility of his taking on another salesperson. The account manager is keen to get the extra resource, since he knows that there is more business in his account if he could cover the ground more effectively. Sally is happy to find the money for the new person, but has to be convinced that she is putting her scarce resources into the most productive area. So, the answer to the first question, "Will you sell more if we put another salesperson on your patch?", is easy: "Sure we will". The second question is much more difficult: "How much more?"

Now consider what is going through the account manager's mind. He knows that if he claims a very high figure, say $5 million, Sally may be sceptical but will probably be sufficiently impressed to let him have the resource. But at what cost. She will, of course, change the estimate into a management objective, and the account manager's target will go up by $5 million or an amount which recognizes that it will take a while to get the new person up to speed. If, on the other hand, the account manager goes low, saying "Well for the first year I think we must allow a settling in period and maybe expect $100 thousand", there are probably other sales managers who will offer Sally a better deal than this and she will prefer to give them the resource. So he has to go somewhere between these two. He wants to be successful and to be seen to be successful. This means that he would rather take a target of $900,000 and make $950,000, than take a target of $1 million and get $950,000. The first is success; the second is failure. And so his thoughts go on. He will try to agree a number which he really believes he can achieve, but will be attractive enough to get Sally's agreement to the hiring of the person.

People normally cover this topic in materials, like this book, which look at the financial side of business. But we must not ignore the fact that most business decisions are made on calculated assessments by experienced people of what will occur if the business takes a certain course of action. The financial side is a great tool to decision making, but a decision-making tool should never be mistaken for the decision itself.

This may seem slightly cynical and to lack some logic, but actually if everyone is competent at their jobs it can work quite well. An experienced sales manager will probably be able to give a reasonable estimate of what his or her resources will bring in. It is, after all, as we have seen in the budgeting chapter, one of the things they are there for. This example is typical of the way parameters for decision making are set and how decisions are discussed and arrived at, particularly in big companies. Middle managers are encouraged to have ideas, to estimate the benefits of the idea and convince their managers that they should be allowed to go ahead. Most are circumspect and cautious about their claims, but some do have a rush of blood to the head and claim huge, but unbelievable, results for their pet project. To deal with both the optimist and the pessimist organizations need a process that examines ideas dispassionately. This is called the *investment appraisal* system and is the main subject of this chapter.

Introduction to investment appraisal

It is an interesting fact that when you are a manager you find that whenever a member of your team asks to see you, as opposed to you asking to see them, they are almost certainly going to ask for resources.

The creation of a business case template is a good start to the investment appraisal process. It helps people know what management are looking for and ensures that new ideas conform with the company's overall strategy. But strategic thinking is only the first part of the system. The rest of the process is defined by the steps

1 Choose a timescale

2 Estimate the benefits

3 Estimate the costs

4 Weigh up the risks to the costs and benefits

5 Produce a projected profit and loss account

6 Produce a cashflow

7 Compare possible projects, along with their risks, with each other and with a benchmark

We will take these one at a time as we examine how companies decide how to invest their resources.

HAR plc

Andy is encouraged by the number of people coming to him with ideas on how they might help to improve things at HAR. They are frequently good ideas that he would like to implement, but always in the first place make things worse by needing resources and spending money, which they do not yet have. "If we could get a presence in Newcastle, I know that my two biggest accounts will put business our way. In a year I reckon I could get up to a turnover of £500,000."

"You know that we could save a lot of energy if we changed out that old boiler for one of those low-energy burners. They are not expensive and have less impact on the environment."

"You know that Tom has resigned. Well, I have talked to him and I think I could get him to change his mind if we could just find a straight 20% increase in his salary."

Andy knows that all these ideas are good, but also that they have no coherence or consistency. He needs new ideas, but he needs them to conform to one or two rules. He decides to think about what would be the ideal case for spending money, and defines what he calls a "business case template". He decides, for example, that he does not want to invest in any project which is not cash neutral within 12 months. It would be ideal if all new expenditure conformed to that. In the end he comes up with four or five criteria by which he will judge all new business ideas.

Choose a timescale

Most investment opportunities need, in the first place, a combination of capital expenditure, which is mainly on fixed assets, and revenue expenditure – money to finance the people and other running costs. Fixed assets have a depreciation period agreed by the finance people to be a reasonable estimate of the productive life of the asset. This depreciation period is frequently the timescale chosen to measure the viability of a project involving capital expenditure.

Compusell Inc.

Compusell's finance department has set a number of company norms for the timescale of justifying fixed assets. It believes that three years is the maximum amount of time that a vehicle will be useful to the company. Plant and machinery is given a much longer life of 5–10 years depending on the speed with which the technologies being purchased are changing. It will be shorter where there is a large element of software involved in the purchase. Computer equipment is difficult. Everyone who is involved in buying this technology knows that something two keystrokes better will be available in the very near future even when you have just made an investment.

The Compusell accountants take a three-year view on computers to be used internally but demand that equipment to be used in providing a service to customers must justify itself within 18 months.

Another element in the decision on timescales is the length of time it takes for the project to get started. It would be less than useful to measure the benefit of building, for example, a tunnel between England and France without taking into account that from inception to operation will take more than ten years. For the finances to work in such a project its revenue earning life will need to be extended to perhaps 50 years.

HAR plc

Andy has a problem. He is aware of two possibilities. Either he can cut the company right back, go back to doing placements himself and recognize that sales turnover in the next year and a half will be a fraction of what it was recently, or he can get more money into the business. With more money he would have a breathing space to put what exists right and make it profitable, and also have a long-term strategy which would involve growing by acquisition. After all, nobody in the recruitment business is immune from this slow down. They are trading well below their best. This means that the price of buying agencies would be very attractive if the business case for the future were strong enough. The economies he has already made allow him time to build the expansionary business case and see if he can interest someone to put in the necessary funds to make it happen. If he allows 12 further months of poor growth, then two years of good growth, he thinks that will represent a sensible view of the way ahead. He decides to base his business case on three years.

In the end timescales for investment appraisal should be sensible. They should reflect the real life of the project, and if it is known at the start that further investment will be required during the time chosen, then that expenditure should be added into the equation.

Estimate the benefits

This is perhaps the most difficult part of the estimating process. As we have seen, it often has an emotional overtone as managers who are making the estimates are aware that these will turn into increased targets or stiffer objectives if the expenditure is approved. It is useful for estimating reasons, and also for risk analysis, as we will see, to break the benefits into four categories.

- Increases in revenue

- Reduction in costs

- Avoidance of future costs

- Improvements in control

Let's take these one at a time.

Increases in revenue

The top line of any proposed profit and loss account is, as we have seen, sales. This is true whether the sales are external, to the company's customers, or internal to other departments within the business. Expenditure of money will often have as the first part of the justification claims that revenues will increase.

HAR Plc

Andy has a lot of experience of what a recruiting executive can earn for the company in a year. He also has good information about the overall productivity of his industry. Sales per employee in the last good year were more than £266,000, with profits per employee at nearly £40,000. This last figure is based on a profit margin of 15% and is, in his opinion, a reasonable benchmark for a good, but not outstanding, year. He believes, as he looks at buying other companies in, that these figures will be produced when the recruiting cycle returns first of all to normal, with the hope that better times may lie ahead. With the timescale he has chosen he is now in a position to estimate the increased revenue and profits coming from acquisitions.

Most times when estimating revenues you will need to use a range of results. The most common method of doing this is to take three possibilities:

- Pessimistic – the lowest outcome which you believe possible

- Most likely – your view of what will actually happen

- Optimistic – the best, but still feasible, outcome

Reduction in costs

In assessing a spending project this area is likely to be very important. Finance people are likely to agree that a reduction of costs is the most tangible benefit there is. You have to make sure that the costs claimed as a reduction are *relevant* costs.

When trying to make a business case the aim is to find sufficient benefits to justify the expense. Most importantly, the manager who will have to take a drop in expenditure budget, since that is how the cost reduction will be realized, must agree any reduction in cost. As we saw with increases in sales, many managers respond very cautiously to an argument that they can do with a lower budget. In the end business cases are well made when reductions in costs outweigh the expenses of the project. Other benefits will make a reasonable case

Selling IT internally

In this example an IT director is trying to cost-justify purchasing the equipment and doing the work to offer a new service to his customers who include the various departments of the oil company, OCC plc, which he works for, and some external prospects. He puts each potential customer into one of four groups depending on the likelihood of their placing an order for the new service. He then makes an estimate of the likely income stream over the next three years allowing for the fact that there may be delays in departments and prospects taking the service up.

	Prospect	Yr 1	Yr 2 and 3
Likelihood 1	Interohm (external)	112.5	150
	Large Gty Bank (external)	162	324
	Technical Department	90	120
	Research Department	64.8	86.4
	Engineering Division	36	48
	Chemicals Division	0	86.4
Total Likelihood 1		465.3	814.8
Likelihood 2	Ranters (external)	112.5	150
	Finance Department	64.8	86.4
	Minerals Division	24	48
Total Likelihood 2		201.3	284.4
Likelihood 3	Oil Division	90	120
	GPD	36	48
Total Likelihood 3		126	168
Likelihood 0	Detergent Division	36	48

From this he can calculate three possibilities for the total stream. This will be the basis for the projected profit and loss account he needs to raise to start the business case. The pessimistic case assumes that only the prospects in likelihood 1 will place an order. The most likely case adds the prospects in likelihood 2, and the optimistic assumes all the prospects will come on board.

Year	1	2	3
Pessimistic (likelihood 1)	465.3	814.8	814.8
Most likely (likelihood 1+2)	666.6	1,099.2	1,099.2
Optimistic (likelihood 1+2+3)	792.6	1,267.2	1,267.2

into a good one. Remember that estimates are not facts; they are negotiable. The agreement of a manager to a small percentage saving in a large cost can have a dramatic effect on the business case. Remember Andy and the 2%.

> **New technology saves space**
>
> A telecommunications manager is trying to cost justify the purchase of a new telephone switchboard for his company. He knows that the new switch has a smaller "footprint" than the old one. The old one took up some 225 square metres, while the new switch will only take up half of that. The accommodation where it sits is very expensive at £300 per square metre. He wants to claim a saving of half of the cost of the accommodation – an impressive £33,750 per annum. But unfortunately this is an unavoidable cost and irrelevant to this telephone replacement project. Unless he can sub-let surplus space, unlikely in this circumstance, or unless the lease was coming up for renewal and he can go elsewhere, he will not be allowed to claim this as a reduction in cost.

Avoidance of future costs

The avoidance of future costs is a slightly different concept to a straightforward reduction in costs. This brings into the business case for a project, costs that would be incurred if the project is not undertaken. Once again, make sure that the cost avoided is real.

HAR plc

In building his business case for expansion, Andy makes the point that expansion will avoid the cost of paying off excess staff. He knows that the only way, apart from expansion, of returning the company to profitability would be to make people redundant. This is an expense in the short term, and, of course, another blow to cashflow.

Improvements in control

Companies are continuously re-engineering their business processes. If they change their strategy in any way or react to changes in technology, they will almost certainly have to review some of their business processes. This almost always ends up with capital and revenue expenditure and is often justified by the fact that it affords management better control over the business. This may be good enough for the people running the business, but it is not sufficiently concrete for the finance department. They want to know how this benefit will turn into cash.

Improvements in control can be difficult to quantify, but if you do not perform this quantification, the finance people will not let you put them in the business case.

Compusell Inc.

Compusell's profits were reduced last year despite an increased turnover. The reason for this was pressure on the gross margin through competitive pricing. This causes the CEO, who knows that the price pressure is not going to ease, to ask managers to examine carefully ways that they might re-engineer business processes and improve profits. One idea under investigation is the cost of holding inventory. It is agreed that the current inventory systems could be tightened to give managers better control by giving them more up-to-date information more quickly. The benefit will come through in one of two ways. Either as increased sales, because inventory is available for delivery when it is required and this will stop some losses to the competition. Or it will come through as a reduced inventory holding.

If the benefit comes through as a 1% increase in sales, they will improve profits by $25 million. If it comes through as a 5% reduction in inventory, then the saving is approximately $20 million.

Estimate the costs

In comparison with benefits, costs are more straightforward to esti-

> **Relevant costs**
>
> The accommodation benefit above is matched in this case by the irrelevance of a cost which might be thought to come into this project equation. Consider a project where a company is considering the installation of a new IT facility. This would be housed in one of the offices currently occupied by administration. Of the three people currently occupying that office, one is due for retirement and will not be replaced, the others can be found a home elsewhere in the administration offices.
>
> Many would suggest that the proposed IT facility should suffer its share of total company rent based on the floor area of the office. This does not make sense. The company are paying exactly the same amount of rent whether they adopt this new project or not. There are no new costs of rent and therefore rent is irrelevant to this decision.

mate. You will find they fall into the categories of staff, equipment rental, depreciation of purchased assets, facilities and consumables. It is always better to agree costs with a supplier, since this removes any risk that they might be wrong. Once again, make sure that the costs are relevant.

In investment appraisal we need to look very carefully at fixed and variable costs to make sure that we do not load irrelevant costs on to

> **A bookshop**
>
> In a bookshop the cost of books sold will vary almost exactly in proportion to sales, whereas salaries, rates, repairs, etc., will change only by steps. These fixed costs are constant in total throughout a particular range of sales. For example, it would be possible to sell a lot more books before it became necessary to take on extra staff.

the project being analysed. The test is whether the costs react to changes in activity level.

In project appraisal, you should not apportion a share of existing fixed costs against new projects. On the other hand, if a new project causes an increase in fixed costs, then the whole of that increase is a relevant cost of the project.

Weigh up the risks to the costs and benefits

We have said that no estimate for the future will be exact: there will always be the unexpected as well as the normal tolerance to be expected in a prediction. Before you move to the step of producing the estimated profit and loss account, take time out to look at the risks to the benefits and costs. The benefits may be less than you predicted, or they may not occur in the timescale predicted. The costs may be greater than budget, either because your estimate is wrong, or because delay has cost money. We will look first at risk analysis methods which can be undertaken at this stage, and then at the end of the chapter at sensitivity analysis and the risk matrix used after you have made your profit and loss and cashflow predictions.

We have already seen one of the ways of taking risk into account, which is to produce a range of forecasts: pessimistic, most likely and optimistic. Let's take that technique a step further, with the use of a risk matrix.

Another method of risk analysis is to take the extremes of each scenario and somehow combine them to give a sensible estimate. We have already seen this in the way that Sally does her sales forecasts.

Compusell Inc.

Let's go back to the inventory system opportunity. We said that there is, as a rule of thumb, an opportunity to increase profits by $25 million if we use

> **Risk matrix**
>
> Remember the types of benefit we identified. Here is another example of a risk matrix using the benefit type as the grouping.
>
> | | Pessimistic | Most likely | Optimistic |
> |---|---|---|---|
> | Reduce costs | 1 | 3 | 6 |
> | Avoid costs | 2 | 5 | 8 |
> | Increase revenues or control | 4 | 7 | 9 |
>
> Experience allows us to give each cell in the matrix a number from 1–9 in the order of confidence that we should have that the benefit will be achieved. It goes from the most likely to occur, the pessimistic estimate for a cost reduction, to the least likely, an optimistic estimate for a benefit in increased sales or improvement in control.
>
> Assuming we know the costs involved in the project, we can now calculate whether this is a high- or low-risk project. Add up all the benefits from the cells marked 1–3. If that produces a number which is greater than the costs, then the project can be termed low risk. If you have to go down to 8 or 9 before the costs are covered, you have a project which carries a high risk of not being profitable.
>
> Don't forget that the objective of risk analysis is not only to identify what the risks are, but also to do something about them. If, for example, there was some doubt about the benefits in cell 5, and that doubt was the difference between a medium- and a high-risk project, you might be inclined to do some more investigation to improve the estimate, or resolve to put extra resources into making sure that during the implementation of the project the benefits in that cell are actually realized.

better inventory techniques to increase sales. We also said that there was a potential cost reduction of $20 million if the benefits of the new system came through as reduction in inventory. In fact we know that neither of these will happen, and that the likelihood is a combination of the two. We could in the risk analysis step combine these two and take forward to the profit and loss account ($25 million/2) + (£20 million/2) or $22.5 million. Not accurate in detail but a good estimate to take into the next step.

The simplest way of ameliorating the risk of under-budgeting is to put contingency money into both the start-up costs of a project and the continuing revenue spend. Many companies build contingency into their investment appraisal technique as a norm. So, you have to put into the profit and loss account an extra 10% capital spend for contingency, and an extra 10% contingency on the running costs.

Produce a projected profit and loss account

Take another look at the internal IT example. Let us assume that management do not like projects that require the optimistic forecasts of benefits in order to make a convincing business case. We only need, then, to produce the profit and loss accounts for the most likely outcome and for the pessimistic forecast. In the profit and loss account we will allow for depreciation of the fixed asset over the three-year life of the project. The accountants have told us to handle depreciation as follows. The capital costs of 1,711 should be spread over the three years, but they have agreed that there will be a residual value of the equipment at the end of that time. This value they have allowed to be 15%. Depreciation is therefore the total cost of the asset minus 15% divided over the three years.

Given that, here is what the two profit and loss accounts will look like.

Projected profit and loss account based on most likely income

	Year 1	Year 2	Year 3
Expenditure			
Staff	70.0	70.0	70.0
Maintenance	0.0	35.0	35.0
Depreciation	485.0	485.0	486.0
Accommodation	18.0	18.0	18.0
Electricity	15.0	15.0	15.0

Sundries	43.0	43.0	43.0
Total	631.0	666.0	667.0
Income (see page 166)	666.6	1,099.2	1,099.2
Profit	35.6	433.2	432.2
Cashflow	520.6	918.2	918.2

Projected profit and loss account based on pessimistic income

	Year 1	Year 2	Year 3
Expenditure (as before)	631.0	666.0	667.0
Income (see page 166)	465.3	814.8	814.8
Profit	−165.7	148.8	147.8
Cashflow	319.3	633.8	633.8

The profit and loss account does not contain any contingency money for costs. The reason for this is that the risks in predicting the income stream so far outweigh any possible additional expenditure on the cost side that it renders it irrelevant. We will judge this project on the likelihood of the income stream providing a viable business. Notice how we have converted the profit and loss into a cashflow at the end. The only difference between the two in this example is depreciation, which is added back to the bottom line to give the cashflow. The capital will be spent before the start of the process, and we will look after that in the last step of the investment appraisal process.

Produce a cashflow

We have already seen how it is possible for a company to be making profits but failing for lack of cash. The major reason for this is that the profit and loss account will show the cost of fixed assets being spread over a period of time by depreciation, whereas when a company buys a fixed asset, the cash has to be paid out immediately. For this reason companies will always look at cashflow forecasts as well as the projected profit and loss account when considering the future.

Similarly, when we appraise an individual project we need to consider the effect on both cash and profit.

A very important point is that we are trying to consider the effect of a new project on a company. Establishing how the company would perform without the new project and comparing this with how it would perform with the new project will assist managers to make the correct decision. It is not correct to compare performance before and after the introduction of the project since changes may be due to other factors.

This brings us to a more general question as to which cashflows are relevant when evaluating a new project. The general principle is that a cash flow is only relevant in evaluating a project if it changes as a result of the introduction of that project. We have already seen some of the effects of this in terms of making sure that you are dealing with relevant costs and benefits.

How we do it

Essentially converting a budgeted profit and loss account into a cashflow forecast is a matter of considering the timing of payments.

If we are preparing monthly budgets and cashflow, then there will be a lot of differences as shown in following table.

Item	Profit and loss account	Cashflow
Sales revenue	include when sold	include when cash is collected
Cost of sales	match with sales	not applicable

Purchases	not applicable	allow for the purchase to be made some time before the sale, but recognize that payment is made some time after purchase
Depreciation	according to policy	not applicable
Fixed assets	not applicable	include when paid for
Other expenses and interest	include on accruals basis, i.e. when incurred	include when paid

When, however, we look at longer-term projects we do not often attempt to budget on a monthly, or even quarterly, basis. It is more usual to produce annual cashflows. In this case, most of the differences between cashflow and profit are ignored with the exception of depreciation.

Compare possible projects, along with their risks, with each other and with a benchmark

Before coming to the main method used by most business people to calculate return on investment, discounted cashflow, take a quick look at the other methods used.

Payback period

This method measures the length of time from the first payment of cash until the total receipts of cash from the investment equals the total payment made on that investment. It does not in any way attempt to measure the profitability of the project and restricts all calculations to a receipts and payments basis.

> **Payback period**
>
> In considering alternative projects, it is the one with the shortest payback period which is preferred.
>
> | | Project 1 | Project 2 |
> |---|---|---|
> | Asset cost | £10,000 | £15,000 |
> | Net cashflow | | |
> | Year 1 | 2,000 | 3,000 |
> | Year 2 | 3,000 | 4,000 |
> | Year 3 | 3,000 | 6,000 |
> | Year 4 | 4,000 | 8,000 |
> | Year 5 | 10,000 | 2,000 |
> | Payback period | 3.5 years | 3.25 years |
>
> In this case the second project would be preferred despite the fact that the positive cashflow for project 1 ramps up in the fifth year.

The payback method has the advantage of being quick and simple, but it has two major disadvantages as well:

- It considers only cash received during the payback period and ignores anything received afterwards.

- It does not take into account the dates on which the cash is actually received. Thus it is possible to have two projects both costing the same, with the same payback period, but with different cashflows.

The payback method has some disadvantages, but is still in use for quite complex projects. This is particularly true where there is a great deal of early capital investment in infrastructure followed by a lengthy period of income derived from those assets. A telephone operator is a good example of such a company.

The payback method giving poor advice

In this example the two projects have the same payback period. However, it is obvious that, without any further information, we should prefer project 2 since the cash is received earlier, and can therefore be reinvested in another project to earn more profits.

	Project 1	Project 2
Asset cost	£10,000	£10,000
Net cashflow		
Year 1	1,000	3,000
Year 2	3,000	3,000
Year 3	3,000	3,000
Year 4	3,000	1,000
Year 5	4,000	4,000
Payback period	4 years	4 years

It is in fact very difficult to know which of these projects is better for the business simply by using the payback method of investment appraisal.

Getting such a lot of large figures down to just two or three crucial ones shows the payback method of investment appraisal being very useful in decision making.

Smart test 23: the PTV Cable Television Company

A cable operator was planning its move into telephony. It was already a successful operator of its television franchise and had a predicted cashflow as shown in Figure 7.1.

- When do the annual cashflows of this enterprise go positive?
- When does the project break even?

	Year 1	Year 2	Year 3	Year 4	Year 5	Year 6	Year 7	Year 8	Year 9	Year 10
Cashflow (000s)	−55,610	−25,283	−27,308	−25,635	−15,466	22,056	34,060	42,716	50,249	58,919
Net cashflow to date	−55,610	−80,893	−108,201	−133,836	−149,302	−127,246	−93,186	−50,470	−221	58,698

Figure 7.1 Television cashflow.

Now look at what happens when the telephony cashflow is calculated, as shown in Figure 7.2.

The answers to the same questions asked about television are that the annual cashflows go positive in year 6 also for telephony, and the break-even date for telephony happens in year 8.

Suppose the business case template for the company included the criteria "Any new project in addition to television must not delay the time that the company has a positive cashflow, and must not delay when the project reaches break even." In both cases this project conforms.

- How much money will the company have to have available to fund the television project?

- How much additionally will it need to go into telephony?

	Year 1	Year 2	Year 3	Year 4	Year 5	Year 6	Year 7	Year 8	Year 9	Year 10
Total revenue	0	2,312,430	9,078,105	18,208,411	28,959,467	36,607,290	39,151,025	41,453,356	43,891,662	46,474,006
Interconnect charges	0	1,331,776	5,237,458	10,565,948	16,917,647	21,457,301	22,985,321	24,375,933	25,850,676	27,414,642
Billing costs	0	188,370	733,466	1,422,455	2,170,951	2,689,880	2,852,903	2,995,548	3,145,325	3,302,592
Administration cost	0	1,077,492	1,929,373	3,067,009	4,401,236	5,365,280	5,719,148	6,046,479	6,392,680	6,758,845
Total costs	0	2,597,638	7,900,297	15,055,413	23,489,834	29,512,460	31,557,372	33,417,960	35,388,682	37,476,079
Operating cashflow	0	−285,207	1,177,808	3,152,999	5,469,633	7,094,830	7,593,653	8,035,396	8,502,981	8,997,927
Capital expenditure	0	9,008,514	7,190,271	6,422,786	7,899,653	583,097	0	0	0	0
Cashflow (000s)	0	−9,293,721	−6,012,463	−3,269,787	−2,430,020	6,511,733	7,593,653	8,035,396	8,502,981	8,997,927
Net cashflow to date	0	−9,293,721	−15,306,184	−18,575,972	−21,005,991	−14,494,259	−6,900,606	1,134,790	9,637,771	18,635,698

Figure 7.2 Telephony cashflow.

Return on capital employed (ROCE)

It can be argued that an improved version of payback is arrived at if you average out the benefits stream over the life of the project. That is what the return on capital employed does.

> **Return on capital employed**
>
> | | |
> |---|---:|
> | Asset cost | £10,000 |
> | Estimated residual value | nil |
> | Expected earnings (before depreciation) | |
> | Year 1 | 2,000 |
> | Year 2 | 3,000 |
> | Year 3 | 5,000 |
> | Year 4 | 7,000 |
> | Year 5 | 8,000 |
> | Total | £25,000 |
> | Net earnings over 5 years | £15,000 |
> | Average earnings | £3,000 |
> | Average RoCE | 30% (3,000/10,000) |

It is sometimes argued that the average capital employed £5,000 should be used instead of £10,000. On this basis, the answer to the previous example would be 60%. Either method can be employed as long as this is done consistently.

Once again, however, RoCE has the disadvantage that it does not take into account the time when the return is received. Thus it is possible to have two projects having the same RoCE but one project starts immediately, and the other has a pre-production period of, say, two years.

Discounted cashflow

We are agreed, then: we need a method of investment appraisal that

> **When would you like the money?**
>
> Suppose we offer to give you $1,000. Would you prefer to have it now or in five years' time? Obviously now, since if you want to spend the money it will be worth more now than it will be after five years of even modest inflation. But what if you don't need to spend it now? Then you still want the use of it so that you could put it somewhere it will earn money. You will therefore have more to spend in five years' time.
>
> But, you have assumed that we are paying no interest in the five years. Suppose we say that if you take it in five years we will pay you 50% per annum interest. Now, of course, you would prefer to wait. In five years we will give you $7,593.75. Even if you needed to spend the money now, you could borrow it and still have a hefty profit in five years.
>
> The concept of discounted cashflow is based on the usefulness of being able to calculate what interest percentage we would have to pay you for it to make no difference at all whether you take the money now or in five years. We know it is somewhere between 0 and 50%.

takes into account the timing of the cashflows as well as their absolute amount. Discounted cashflow does just that. Look at it this way.

The mechanics of discounted cashflow

To arrive at a method of doing this, consider the following: You have inherited £10,000 from Aunt Mary. Unfortunately, she had heard that you are liable to spend money fairly freely so the will says that you cannot receive the cash until your 30th birthday. You are 27 today. (Happy Birthday!)

Aunt Mary was actually fairly well informed. You are desperate to get this money before lunchtime tomorrow in order to place a bet on a horse someone has told you is going to do well in the 2.30 race.

You have found a friendly banker who will advance you part of the money.

The interest rate is 10% per annum and she is prepared to advance you an amount A such that with interest you will owe the bank exactly £10,000 in three years' time. How much can you get?

If you borrow £100 now, you will owe interest of £10 by the end of one year, so the total outstanding will be £110.

During the second year, interest will be charged on the total amount outstanding of £110, i.e. interest of £11. The total outstanding would be £121.

During the third year, interest will be charged on the total amount outstanding of £121, i.e. interest of £12.10. The total outstanding would then be £133.10.

We can see therefore that for every £100 borrowed, £133.10 must be repaid.

Therefore, solving the equation:

$$A \times 1.331 = £10,000$$

will tell us how much can be borrowed now, i.e. about £7,510. This technique can of course be generalized to deal with any rate of interest and any time period.

We can now develop a method to compare two projects. Cashflows due in the future may be converted to equally desirable cashflows due today using the above method. This technique is know as discounting and the equivalent cashflow due today is known as a present value.

Timing of cashflow	Amount of cashflow	Discount factor at 10%	Present value
Immediate	(10,000)	1	(10,000)
After 1 year	3,000	0.909	2,727
After 2 years	4,000	0.826	3,304
After 3 years	5,000	0.751	3,755
After 4 years	3,000	0.683	2,049
Net present value (NPV)			£1,835

Discount factors may be found from tables or by using the formula:

$$\text{Discount factor} = 1/(1 + i)^n$$

where i = discount rate and n = number of years.

In particular, consider the discount factor used above for year 3, i.e. 0.751. When deciding how much we could borrow from the bank in respect of Aunt Mary's bequest we divided £10,000 by 1.331. It is an exactly equivalent calculation to multiply £10,000 by 0.751 – the discount factor for 3 years at 10%.

The final result takes into account all cashflows by totalling them, and is known as the net present value (NPV) of the project.

If compelled to choose between two projects, we will select the one with the higher NPV. If we have a large number of projects, all of which can be undertaken, then we would wish to invest in every project with a positive NPV.

Comments on using discounted cashflows

1 The initial investment occurs at time 0, the start of the project. Further cashflows then arise throughout the first year but all of these are combined to give one figure for the whole year. This one net cashflow is then treated as though it all arose on the first anniversary of the initial investment. Similarly, all of the cashflows during the second year are combined to give the year 2 cashflow, and so on.

If it is absolutely necessary to make the calculations more accurate, cashflows could be allocated to shorter periods (e.g. quarters) and the appropriate discount factors used.

However, most companies would not consider it worthwhile to use shorter periods because the extra accuracy achieved is hardly worthwhile bearing in mind that all of the data is estimated. Further, combining all of the cashflows into one usually results in a more cautious approach to project appraisal, that is it tends to diminish the NPV.

2 Cashflows must be relevant costs and benefits as explained previously.

3 The discount rate represents the cost of capital. In a large company the treasury function will lay this down.

> **Know the ground rules**
>
> If you work for a large company and are involved in investment appraisal, make sure that you know what their discount factor is. It may be the same as its notional cost of capital or it may be much higher. Some companies want technology projects to give a positive NPV when tested against a discount factor of 15% or greater.

> **IRR**
>
> Would you rather have 10% of $50 million, or 20% of $5 million? An easy question, but if you make decisions based only on the IRR, you may well opt for the second. Always use the NPV for decision making.

4   Projects with a positive NPV add to the value of the company and if they are OK against other business case template criteria should generally be accepted.

5   There is another numerical concept called the internal rate of return or IRR. Remember the question "When would you like to be given $1,000?" We said then that it was possible to work out an interest rate that would make it completely immaterial whether you took the money now or later. This is the IRR, the discount factor at which the NPV is reduced to zero.

You may think that the above is so simplified that there is much

> **Smart test 24: discounted cashflows**
>
> To practise basic discounting, complete the following table.
>
> A company has the following project under consideration:
>
> | Timing of cashflow | Amount of cashflow | Discount factor at 15% | Present value |
> |---|---|---|---|
> | Immediate | (20,000) | | |
> | After 1 year | 10,000 | | |
> | After 2 years | 8,000 | | |
> | After 3 years | 6,000 | | |
> | Net present value | | | |

more to learn before you can use the technique in practice. This is not so. The difficulty is in establishing the cashflows that should go into the computation. Once this has been done, the mechanics do not change whether we are dealing with the Channel Tunnel or buying a simple machine. We are now in a position to take investment appraisal one step further. You will remember the oil company and the cashflows we had calculated.

Projection based on most likely income

Year	1	2	3
Cashflow	520.6	918.2	918.2

Projection based on pessimistic income

Year	1	2	3
Cashflow	319.3	633.8	633.8

To maintain realism our discounted cashflow must take account of the tax liability that will arise. You always need the accountants to help with such a calculation. Every company is different and the tax treatment of such a project is hard to predict if you are an accountant closely involved with the company's tax position and impossible if you are not.

In this case we have been told to use a tax rate of 35%. Where there is a positive cashflow it comes through to the company as an addition to profits. Such profits are, of course, taxable. In cashflow terms the cash implications of tax occur the year after the liability, since they occur after the end of the company year when the company has worked out its profits and the tax implications. So, since the project has a positive cashflow in year 1 of £521, it will have a cash outflow for tax in year 2 of 35% of £521 which is £182.

There is one further tax complication. The capital expenditure for this project is £1,711 (always working in £000s) and the way that is treated for tax is different. No matter how a company's accountants and auditors decide to treat depreciation for profit and loss account purposes, the tax authorities have their own method. So far we have talked about the straight-line method of depreciation where an asset is depreciated by a fixed amount for each of the years of its usefulness; the tax authorities use another method called *reducing balance*. With this method the asset is depreciated by a set percentage each year with the balance carried forward to the next year. In this case the initial value of the asset is £1,711. This is reduced by 25% of the reducing balance each year. So, 25% of £1,711 is £428 and the tax rate of 35% therefore gives a tax benefit in year 2 of £149.8, rounded up in the cashflow to £150. The value carried forward is £1,711 minus £428, which is £1,283; 25% of that figure is £321 and 35% of that is £112. At the end of year 3 the asset is sold and tax is allowed at 35% on the difference between the proceeds £257 and the tax written-down value of £962.

Notice how you require year 4 to take into account the tax payments even though the project is being measured over 3 years.

Cashflow forecast: most likely outcome

Year	0	1	2	3	4
Capital	(1,711)			257	
Tax capital allowances			150	112	247
Operating cashflow		521	918	918	
Tax			(182)	(321)	(321)
Cashflow	(1,711)	521	886	966	(74)
Discount factors 7%	1	0.93	0.87	0.82	0.76
Present value	(1,711)	484	771	792	(57)
Net present value	279				

Year	0	1	2	3	4
Written-down value		1,711	1,283	962	
Capital allowance		428	321		
Balancing allowance				705	

Cashflow forecast: pessimistic outcome

Year	0	1	2	3	4
Capital	(1,711)			257	
Tax capital allowances			150	112	247
Operating cashflow		319	634	634	
Tax			(112)	(222)	(222)
Cashflow	(1,711)	319	672	781	25
Discount factors 7%	1	0.93	0.87	0.82	0.76
Present value	(1,711)	297	584	641	19
Net present value	(170)				
Written-down value		1,711	1,283	962	
Capital allowance		428	321		
Balancing allowance				705	

The NPV for the pessimistic outcome is negative at (170), while that for the most likely is positive at 279. The main difference between the two cashflows are the customers with the likelihood of 2. There are a number of things we can do about this. We can go back to the main likelihood 2 prospects and try and close them off in one way or another: either get them to sign up or at least appear much more positive about signing up, or cross them off the list. The removal of uncertainty greatly increases the chances of making a good decision. Putting resources into these prospects may involve removing them from the likelihood 3 candidates. But this is no problem because we can get to a viable project without them and maybe come to see them as the icing on the cake once the project has been implemented and successful to the most likely estimate.

More about risk analysis

We have had a look at risk analysis in terms of weighting the likelihood of benefits occurring and costs being overrun. There are a number of useful techniques at this later stage in the process where we use the cashflows created to assess further risk.

Sensitivity analysis

Having gone through the process of understanding the rules and raising your profit and loss account and cashflow, you, the prospective project owner, get further benefits. At this stage you know whether, using the hurdle rate set as a company norm, your project is viable. You also know how it matches up to alternative ways of spending the money – an NPV of $41 million is better than one of $38 million. Now you can use the cashflow for sensitivity analysis or asking the "what if?" question. To be more precise we can take each uncertainty in the inputs and ask the questions

- What is the effect on the NPV if this input changes?

- How far can the input change before the NPV falls to zero?

Using sensitivity analysis helps to identify whether the project is likely to go wrong because of its sensitivity to key inputs. It also tells management which are the key inputs and therefore the ones to be most closely watched once the project is implemented.

> **A telephony service**
>
> Suppose you are supplying a telephony service and need to test a discounted cashflow against its sensitivity to the number of users of a new switchboard you intend to invest in. You have created a discounted cashflow using the number 5,500 as the number of users. If you had the cashflow on a spreadsheet you could find out what the NPV would be if there were in fact 5,400 users. Similarly, you could find out the number of users you could drop to before the NPV goes negative. You are testing the model for its sensitivity to this parameter, and could repeat the exercise for any parameter, whether it affects costs or benefits.

Expected value analysis

In this technique, each variable is given a range of possible values with associated probabilities. Consider the following rather simple example, based on the telephony service described above.

You might decide that the number of users of the new exchange is not certain to be 5,500 but that there is only a 60% chance of this number being correct. Let us suppose that there is a 40% chance of the number of users being 4,800. The NPV of each outcome has been calculated as shown below.

We now work out the following:

No. of users	NPV (x)	Probability (p)	xp
4,800	60,444	0.4	24,178
5,500	684,248	0.6	410,549
Expected value			434,727

This expected value is simply the weighted average of the separate outcomes. If the project to introduce a new telephone system was undertaken 1,000 times, then we would expect the demand to be 4,800 on approximately 400 occasions and 5,500 on approximately 600 occasions. The average return would be the figure quoted above.

You can see from this explanation that this approach is not likely to be very helpful for a capital project that is only undertaken once. The resulting expected value will never actually occur, one of the outcomes in the NPV column will occur – but we don't know which.

If you have trouble with the above, consider the average family size in Europe. We could say that the average number of children in a family is 2.2. This average is simply not useful in predicting how many children any household will have. Indeed we can be absolutely certain that no household will have the average.

So when is expected value useful? Companies use it when they face the same decision over and over again.

> **Oil probabilities**
>
> For example, OCC Oil has to evaluate exploration decisions based on the costs and revenues and the probability of success. If they use expected value analysis consistently for all such decisions, then, in the long run, on average, they will make the correct decisions.

Optimistic/most likely/pessimistic estimates

We have seen this method in assessing benefits. Here it is again at the end of the process. Management are asked to make three predictions for each input: an optimistic prediction, a most likely outcome and a pessimistic prediction. The NPV on each set of assumptions is then computed, as follows, again using our telephony company:

Input	Optimistic	Most likely	Pessimistic
No. of users	6,000	5,500	4,500
Mark-up on calls	4%	2%	1%
Staff cost inflation	6%	8%	11%
Rental per user: increase	+10%	0	−5%
NPV	£1,785,197	£684,248	£–498,196

This method can be used on its own – in which case management have an idea of the likely limits to the returns. Alternatively, it can be combined with the expected value analysis method, when probabilities are allocated to each set of assumptions and a single expected value is worked out.

8 Getting Money into a Business

Introduction

The last chapter looked at the long term from an individual project's point of view. This chapter looks at the financing of the whole enterprise and starts from refreshing your memory about the absolute basics of how cash gets into a company and the implications of different sources of money. We have seen how investors plan what shares to include in their portfolios. Now let us think about the opposite of this – how managers get the money they require to run the business. Shareholders don't give money to everyone, you know, they look for the smart folk.

How cash comes into a business

The two sources of long-term finance in a business are share capital and loan capital. Share capital comes in as cash when the initial owners of the business first buy their shares. The owners will probably at the outset be the founders of the business and intrepid venture capitalists, either private like the founder's Dad, or public such as venture capital funds.

The implications of the two types of capital are different. In one sense share capital is cheaper. Return on the shareholders' capital comes in the shape of dividends that are normally paid twice a year. In the early stages of a business the owners may very well drop the requirement for dividends and allow the managers to keep all the profits in the business for expansion. At that stage the money could be said to be free.

> **Attracting share capital**
>
> To attract share capital into a new business, the board needs a credible business plan that promises a return commensurate with the risk of failure.

There is also no necessity for the managers to plan to have the cash to buy the shares back. In practical terms the money is in the company for ever. The only downside in using share capital to get a business going is the cost of the operation; lawyers and accountants do not come cheap. Oh, and you have to find someone happy to take the risk of putting money into a business that may very well fail with the consequent loss of the entire capital injection. It is this risk of failure which makes shareholders demand, in the long term, that their overall returns should be higher than the providers of loans. They get this return through the growth of dividends, which they can take, as we have seen, in the dividends themselves in the long term or in the short-term growth in the capital value of the shares.

Loan capital is probably cheaper to arrange. It comes from banks and financial institutions that measure the risk of the company and then charge an interest rate to reflect that risk. There is a huge irony here.

If someone offered to lend you £10 for a week, but asked you to agree to pay back twice that amount at the time of repayment, you would not need to have read this book to realize that that is a bad

> **Growing the share price**
>
> To improve the share price the board needs a track record of paying a predictable and increasing dividend, or in high-growth industries the potential to do this in the future. In either case they will be in a position to attract further share capital into the business at the higher price to fund other ideas for expansion.

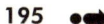

Smart test 25

If inflation is running at 2.2% per annum and you are being charged 9.8% for an overdraft, what is the real rate of interest you are paying?

deal. Suppose, however, that you are completely broke and know that you will have £71 in cash by the day at which you have to make the capital and 100% interest repayment – still not interested? Ah, we forget to mention that your two children have not eaten for 36 hours and that they are wailing for food. It is in circumstances like these that the loan-sharks of inner- city sink estates make such loans and prosper. This is a good starting point for considering the purveyors of loan capital.

Their view is that they tailor their interest charges to protect themselves against the risk of default. The more difficult the situation the borrower is in, the higher the risk, and therefore the higher the price of help.

If you are running a huge conglomerate and wish to borrow $250 million to buy up a subsidiary in another country, you will be wined and dined by various money-lenders eager to get your business at less than 1% above the rate at which the banks themselves borrow money. If you need £20,000 to tide your cornershop over a refurbishment, you will probably have to trawl the high street to find a lender willing to lend you the money at 5 or 6% above bank rate. And they will probably want you to back the security of the loan by remortgaging your house. Banks are indeed the people who lend umbrellas to small businesses only when it is not raining.

With loan capital you have to plan the repayments to keep within the agreed contract when the loan was made.

> **Attracting loan capital**
>
> Banks give the impression that they are only interested in how certain they are to get their money back.

Getting non-equity capital into a business

The sources of finance are different depending on the size of the business that is raising capital. The following are available to any company but are particularly relevant to small and medium-sized businesses whether they are already listed on the stock market or not.

HAR Plc

Andy has made a good start to the short-term problems at HAR. He has made everyone in the company conscious of the problem, and got them to work hard at improving all their financial results even if only by a small percentage. He has moved a number of costs from fixed to variable. He is still losing money but in a manner that is seen to be under control.

His short-term business plan has been achieved and the credibility this has given him has kept the banks at bay, at least for the moment. But his interest bill is crippling and getting worse. Short-term money, loans and overdraft, are costing 10% per annum and in some cases more. He decides to look for alternative ways of financing his short-term requirement and turns to factoring.

Factoring companies will, as it were, buy the trade debtors of a company. They will supply a service that includes keeping the whole sales ledger, doing the company's invoicing, guaranteeing debt and chasing for payment. Andy does not want their services beyond financing his debtors. This has the impact of bringing some £3 million into the company. There is a snag. The bank that is the main lender of short-term funds has made a number of conditions. One of these is that the overdraft must not exceed 60% of trade debtors. This means that Andy has to repay the overdraft, and will no longer have access to that very flexible type of finance. However, since the price of the overdraft is much higher than factoring, and since he is getting the company under control with its budgets realistic, he is happy to do this. In many ways it is a good move to remove or dramatically reduce the overdraft. Overdraft money has the benefit of flexibility in that you only pay interest for money borrowed on a dayto- day basis. But as a long-term source of funds it is expensive, and also inflexible: if the bank for any or no reason gets concerned about the loan it can recall it instantly – that's the deal. Overdraft is always mentioned as a source of short-term funds and should be treated that way.

By these actions Andy has secured the short term, 1–3 month, survival of the company.

If a company has no covenant on the debtors, then factoring may very well have no impact whatever on its ability to raise loan finance.

Other forms of short-term capital include term loans, which are loans for a fixed period of time and will normally also come from a bank. You can also squeeze your creditors and do deals with them which give you more time to pay. There may well be a charge for this but at least with some suppliers you may be an important customer, which gives you a little bit of muscle. Most other forms, such as bankers' acceptance facility, are variations on the overdraft.

If you cannot use a spreadsheet package with reasonable skill – enough, say, to build a cashflow from scratch – you are putting your-

A small business

The key to borrowing short term is for a small business to plan it long term. Make sure that your cashflows tell the truth, then allow for the situation being worse than that. Predict sensibly far ahead, but at least one year in detail. Organize the facility well in advance and run your accounts impeccably. Never go over an overdraft limit without authority.

Given that you do this for a while you will build a track record, so that when you decide you are going to need extra money to do something new, you go into a positive environment at the bank rather than a suspicious one.

Bankers, like shareholders, hate surprises and uncertainty, so don't give them any.

self at a disadvantage whether you are in a big company or small. In such circumstances you are working in the position of a manager in the 1970s. At that time managers wanted to ask the "What if?" question to test out risk and results in various combinations of eventualities. They knew that a new product broke-even in two years if the sales came in on plan, but they did not know, on the down side, at what point the lack of sales would start to threaten the cashflow of the company or the department involved. They did not know, on the upside, when higher than expected sales would push the production people into further investment. But mainly they found it difficult to have a comfortable level of information to compare one investment project with another when the type of investment was very different. They needed to be able to ask an infinite number of "What if?" questions.

Various pieces of applications software were written and experimented with, but it was not until the launch of the first spreadsheet system, Visicalc, in the late 1970s that managers received the ability to create the models they wanted, and to break free from their reliance on the finance department to measure, probably to five decimal places, the financial outcome of the inspired guesses managers make when estimating the future. Computers opened up a totally new planning environment.

The move from dependency on the finance department is rendered useless, of course, if it leads to a new dependency on the computer department. Out of the prying department into the technical mire, you might say. Here also spreadsheets offered, and continue to do so, a simple-to-use mechanism which allows functional managers to create their own models to meet exactly the problem they are trying to solve. Spreadsheets are the antithesis of the general-purpose computer system which solves part of everyone's problem but fails everybody in some way.

The use of the words "simple" and "computers" in combination always needs careful examination, an IBM executive once described a computer as "as user friendly as a cornered rat", but the spreadsheet genuinely can be simple to use. It can then be stretched in a thousand ways to offer complex solutions to complex problems. People who keep learning about them and using them find that they are using not just an upmarket calculating machine capable of producing models, but a powerful programming language of immensely wide value. In fact even seasoned spreadsheet modellers after some years are still aware that they are only using a fraction of the power of the tool.

HAR plc: the long-term strategy

Having solved the short term, Andy now looks ahead. In his judgement HAR has a brighter future than a number of its competitors. HAR is pretty well placed to take advantage of the business upturn when it comes. He is sure that he could build a good business case for combining a few companies together under the HAR umbrella if he could attract the capital to make it happen. He has sounded out one company through an intermediary. This is a business owned by its founder who is nearing retirement age. The founder has said that if Andy can offer a plan for merging the businesses, looking after the managers who work for him at present and getting the new entity on to the stock market, he will consider it carefully.

So, the long term has an aim – to float a company in, say, three years' time and to build it by further acquisition.

So much for short-term money. Medium-term finance for a business can be defined as 1–3 year money:

Bank loans, of course, secured or unsecured, can also be used as medium-term money, but there are others:

- Leasing and hire purchase are methods of spreading the payments for an asset. There is a finance charge for this, the equivalent of interest, and it can be quite high if the asset is in demand or reasonably low when the suppliers are looking for customers. Car manufacturers, for example, give very good terms for leasing their cars when the car market is sluggish.

- Check for government grants that are available for various reasons to do with innovation or the region where jobs will be created. The only downside on these is the amount of paperwork that goes into the application, and the monitoring which the government department will put into the project once it has started. Both of these consume a lot of management time.

- Loan guarantee scheme. In this arrangement government provides a guarantee to the clearing banks that lend to small businesses. It is specifically for medium-term finance and will have a limit, currently 70% of loans up to £100,000. The cost of this is that the business pays a premium for the guarantee of 1 or 2%.

We come now to venture capital. Venture capitalists have a fund of money that they put into a series of high-risk enterprises. They look for a new venture which is too risky for traditional bank lending and their finance is often known as 'ground floor' or 'early stage' investment. Since it is high risk it is also expensive, and the owners of the business will have to offer equity in the business to the venture people who will also probably want to put a director on the board.

The venture capitalist will look for an 'exit route' within, say, three years. Remember they only expect 10% of their ventures to blossom. This tends to put them predominantly into the high-technology area where the eventual returns can be huge. Huge is a good word to use in relation to venture capitalists – they want to invest big money in adventurous enterprises.

A venture capitalist

If a board of directors has decided to go to the stock market for capital for the first time or to raise further capital, it is a human reaction to make the raising of capital the objective. It is wiser to concentrate on running an effective business and setting good strategies for the way ahead. At some point the experts in the equity markets will tell when the time and shape of the enterprise is suitable for presentation to investors.

Someone who has had venture capital put into their business

On the other hand, never forget that they are the experts on raising capital and that you, however good you may be at running a business, are a novice. So do your preparation, listen and learn fast and get advice from people who have been in your position as well as the financial community.

HAR plc

Andy speaks to some venture capitalists and finds them interested but only after the first merger has taken place. They want him to find another investor, or business angel, to fund this.

Through the owner of the company he is going to merge with, Andy finds such a person who will put in the necessary funds to buy out a considerable slice of the outgoing owner's company. This will put Andy into the position where, after some negotiation, the claims of all the individuals involved, particularly the people running the new business, in terms of shareholding can be met. Remember at this stage only the owner of the additional business is actually making money. The others are holding shares that may or may not have a value in the future.

The merger has another important value to Andy. To get this far has taken a huge amount of his time. With the managers from the merged business now taking over the day-to-day running of the company, Andy is free to work with the other potential backers of the growing enterprise.

> **Smart rule of thumb**
>
> It takes time to get venture capital. Allow at least six months. It always takes longer than anyone thinks at the outset, and you often have to make compromises to make it happen.

The venture capitalist will try to structure a deal so that the management has a strong incentive to work hard. They may have to put up with modest salaries, lower perhaps than they could get working for someone else. They will also talk of "equity ratchets", whereby there is a transfer of equity from the venture capitalist to the entrepreneurs if performance targets are met, or vice versa if they are not.

For long-term loan capital, small businesses have a variety of options. They can mortgage assets, sell assets and lease them back, or just take out long-term loans. The disadvantages of these are only

> **Leverage**
>
> Suppose a company has profits of £1 million. The owners are willing to sell it for ten times this or £10 million. An entrepreneur buys the business using her own money of £1 million and borrowings of £9 million. Suppose further that the business grows and within two years is running with profits of £2 million. The business is now worth £20 million which, if realized, would pay back the debt and leave the entrepreneur with £11 million as return on the original stake of only £1 million.
>
> Unfortunately it works in reverse as well. If the business struggles and profits drop to £500,000, then the value of the business has gone down to £5 million and it still has debts of £9 million.
>
> Finance leverage increases both the risks and the potential returns.

concerned with interest rates and repayments, the benefit, is to do with our old friend leverage, this time financial leverage.

Raising capital from the capital markets

Capital markets exist for the benefit of companies and investors. In their primary role they enable organizations to raise new long-term finance – this helps companies. In their secondary role they help investors by providing a marketplace for the trading of securities.

Most small listings are issued by placing. The issuer, normally a merchant bank and a stockbroker, place the shares with their clients. Large issues are normally by "offer for sale", or "offer for sale by tender". In the first case the company offers the shares at a price; in the second the shares are sold by auction. In almost all cases the issue is underwritten, which means that financial institutions agree to buy any unsold shares for a fixed fee. This takes the risk out of the share issue as far as the company raising the finance is concerned. It is, of course, very expensive to remove the risk. Their fees are high.

To obtain a listing a company will probably have been trading successfully for at least three years, and have a minimum value which will satisfy the stock markets.

> ### Smart rule of thumb
>
> The legal and financial fees involved in a flotation are high. Expect to pay at least £1 million to raise £10 million
>
> Raising money is more expensive at certain times. It tends to be expensive for a new company and very expensive if you go back for more money because of difficulties in implementing the business plan. If things are going well and you need more money to expand, you will find it costs less.

One of the big advantages of floating is that it makes available a wide range of investors who, if presented with a good business case, will put more money into the business. A rights issue is the most common way of doing this and is so called because the company offers the new shares first of all to existing shareholders, who have the right to buy them and maintain their share of the business and avoid dilution.

> **Don't look at flotation through rose-coloured spectacles**
>
> Since at least 25% of a company's shares must be put on the market for the company to be listed, it follows that the introduction of new capital always dilutes the current shareholders' share in the business. When a company goes public, the current owners own less of the company and have a new set of individuals and institutions to report to. This can be onerous, and some people have found it so onerous that they have taken the company back into private ownership by buying the shares back.
>
> The costs of doing this will be very high for both the floating and the retrieving.

We have spent a lot of time on the equity side of capital markets. There are a number of other ways that companies can raise money in tradable securities apart from equities. Some loan capital is described as *debenture* although there is little of this being issued in the UK at this time. Debentures carry interest which is normally paid half yearly. They are usually issued by a "placing" into financial institutions and only a small proportion is offered to the public.

One of the ways a company can raise money but avoid the cash outflow in interest payments that goes with normal loan capital is to issue discounted bonds. In this case there is a very low interest rate, and the bonds are issued at a lower price than they will be redeemed at when the time comes. This suits the company looking to pay a low rate of interest, and is suitable for some investors since the return comes not in interest but in a capital gain when the bond is redeemed.

Large companies raise short- and medium-term finance by issuing *commercial paper*, a simple promise to pay a fixed sum of money on a fixed date. Sometimes commercial papers carry a normal rate of interest, and sometimes they are discounted. All of these instruments can offer general finance for the business, but are often associated with an actual project, such as the taking over of another company.

Compusell Inc.

On its balance sheet Compusell has notes payable and short-term borrowings of $936 million, but its overwhelming source of long-term finance, like a lot of large, long-established companies, is in the retained earnings section of shareholders' funds.

Compusell has the opposite problem in terms of capital to HAR. They have built up considerable amounts of surplus cash. In fact they have $3,360 million in cash or short-term equivalents of cash. Even if they spend all of this, their current ratio will only go down from its current 1.8 to 1.5, ignoring the positive cashflow it is currently generating.

The board plans to use that cash to buy back its own shares. They plan to buy back shares to the value of $1,500 million. In the short term this will damage their profit and loss account since the interest they will lose is much less than the dividend payments they will save. But there are other advantages. In the long term the dividend would have to have increased at least in line with inflation. They have also improved their earnings per share by decreasing the number of shares, and this will probably have a positive impact on their share price. They care intensely about their share price. One of the benefits of a higher share price is that companies they buy and pay for with their own shares will become cheaper. Since this is a principal plank of their strategy, they make the change in capital structure.

We have looked at how investors value existing companies, and how they look at the risk of new ventures that are trying to attract them. Let's finish with the unusual, some would say extraordinary, way that the market valued internet companies at the end of the 1990s. Such companies had a huge need for capital to get going, but were likely to take four or five years or more before they even sent out an invoice let alone made a profit. It is a neat encapsulation of what this book has discussed.

> **Creative accounting: valuing the long-term future**
>
> The stock market appeared convinced that a large proportion of sales transactions were going to be carried out using the internet. Many companies were changing their selling environments to cater for this, and specialist companies were started with the sole purpose of exploiting this type of selling channel. But how do you value them, when growth is going to take ten years to reach potential?
>
> "Easy", says the market, "Take the market size for the industry sector and project it out ten years. If it is, for example, global transactions in food and drink, then it will be an incredibly high figure in the trillions of dollars. Now look at a company that has started work on developing the systems and customer base to allow these transactions to occur on-line. Some of them have spent hundreds of millions of dollars to get ready. Allow that they, the market leaders of the future, will have a proportion of those transactions, say 10%, and you have another very high number. Assume that they can make a profit of 20% on these sales and allow that that represents their profit stream in ten years' time, still a very large figure.
>
> Now discount that figure back to present value. Use a discount rate of 2–3% above depositor interest rate to allow for risk. That present value now represents what the company would be earning now and can be used as the earnings side of the price earnings ratio. Give it a conservative P/E ratio of 10, which means you multiply it by 10 to get the present value of the business. Since we started in trillions, we are still in billions with this figure."

> This explains how companies such as Amazon.com and eBay.com had market valuations in billions of dollars before they started to make a profit at all. Was the market right? Not for most of the companies that promised so much; but some kept going and are now breaking even or making profits. We proved earlier an argument for buying shares which are out of fashion rather than the subject of huge bull market pressure, but the performance of internet shares suggested the opposite – fill your boots with shares which are showing growth of hundreds of percent per annum, or miss out on the really high returns available on the stock market. OK, we'll say it once more:
>
> **NOBODY SAID FINANCIAL LIFE WAS EASY**

Epilogue

If you only take three points away from reading this book we suggest they are as follows:

- *The 2% rule.* Smart managers are the ones who demonstrate their toughness in spending the company's money. This does not mean that you are mean with the Christmas party, since that could demotivate people and even lose you staff. It means that when you spend a little or a lot, you are aware of what the company is gaining in return.

- *Cash is king.* Even if your role is a long way from the treasury department, think about the implications on cashflow of all decisions. It is smart to let your superiors know that cash is a consideration you take seriously.

- If cash is king, then *customers are the divinity*. The smartest way to improve the bottom line is to increase the top line – sales values. Whether your customers are internal or external listen to what they want, deliver value and charge for it. One of the simplest ways to look smarter than the average manager is deliver reliably to customers, on time and within budget.

HAR and Compusell

So what, finally, of Sally and Andy? You have to hand it to Andy; he is going about a difficult job in a smart way. He considers the financial side of all his decisions and seems to have some empathy with the shareholders. He looks smart enough to succeed; all he needs is the money to implement the strategy. He'll probably get it: people with money are always looking for people who can manage it.

Sally looks less smart. She still has the appearance of running a department for the sales it will produce rather than the profit it will generate. In common with many managers, if she does not overcome this financial blind spot, she may not make it to the very top. Up there money counts, and a smart manager counts money.

Glossary

Accounting concepts The basic assumptions underlying the preparation of accounts, namely "going concern", "accruals", "consistency" and "prudence".

Accounting policies Those principles, bases, conventions, rules and practices judged by the business to be most appropriate to its circumstances and therefore adopted in the preparation of its accounts.

Accounts payable American terminology for creditors.

Accounts receivable American terminology for debtors.

Accrual An expense or a proportion thereof not invoiced prior to the balance sheet date but included in the accounts – sometimes on an estimated basis.

Accruals concept Income and expenses are recognized in the period in which they are earned or incurred, rather than the period in which they happen to be received or paid.

Asset Any property or rights owned by the company that have a monetary value. Recently in some circumstances, assets have been included in company balance sheets if the company controls the asset and without necessarily owning it, e.g. an asset on a finance lease.

Balance sheet A statement describing what a business owns and owes at a particular date.

Borrowing ratio This ratio is important in determining the credit worthiness of the business. It is defined as total debt (short-term and long-term loans) expressed as a ratio of shareholders' funds less intangible assets.

Capital employed The aggregate amount of long-term funds invested in or lent to the business and used by it in carrying out its operation.

Cashflow A statement of future, anticipated cash balances based on estimated cash inflows and outflows over a given period.

Consistency concept The requirement that once an accounting policy for a particular item in the accounts has been adopted the same policy should be used from one period to the next until a new policy is judged more appropriate. Any change in policy must be fully disclosed.

Costs of good sold, also *Cost of sales* Those costs (usually raw materials, labour and production overheads) directly attributable to goods that have been sold. The difference between sales and cost of goods sold is gross profit.

Creditors Amounts due to those who have supplied goods or services to the business.

Current asset An asset which, if not already in cash form, is expected to be converted into cash within 12 months of the balance sheet date.

Current cost The convention by which assets are valued at the cost of replacement at the balance sheet date (net of depreciation for fixed assets).

Current liability An amount owed which will have to be paid within 12 months of the balance sheet date.

Current ratio The ratio of current assets to current liabilities in a balance sheet, providing a measure of business liquidity.

Debentures Long-term loans, usually secured on the company's assets.

Debtors Amounts due from customers to whom goods or services have been sold but for which they have not yet paid.

Deferred asset/liability An amount receivable or payable more than 12 months after the balance sheet date.

Deferred taxation An estimate of a tax liability payable at some estimated future date, resulting from timing differences in the taxation and accounting treatment of certain items of income and expenditure.

Depreciation An estimate of the proportion of the cost of a fixed asset which has been consumed (whether through use, obsolescence or the passage of time) during the accounting period.

Distribution The amount distributed to shareholders out of the profits of the company, usually in the form of a cash dividend.

Dividend cover The ratio of the amount of profit reported for the year to the amount distributed.

Dividend yield The ratio of the amount of dividend per share to the market share price of a listed company.

Earnings per share The amount of profit attributable to shareholders divided by the number of ordinary shares in issue.

Equity gearing This ratio shows the company's total exposure to debt. It is defined as shareholders' funds expressed as a ratio of total liabilities. It is of particular interest to unsecured creditors.

Exceptional item Income or expenditure that, although arising from the ordinary course of business, is of such unusual size or incidence that it needs to be disclosed separately.

Expense A cost incurred, or a proportion of a cost, the benefit of which is wholly used up in the earning of the revenue for a particular accounting period.

Financial Reporting Standards (FRS) Statements issued by the Accounting Standards Board which describe approved methods of accounting.

Fixed asset Asset held for use by the business rather than for sale.

Fixed cost A cost that does not vary in proportion to changes in the scale of operations, e.g. rent.

Gearing Gearing is the word used to describe the financing of the company in terms of the proportion of capital provided by shareholders (equity) compared with the proportion provided by loan capital (debt).

Gearing ratios There are many different ways to measure gearing. The commonest is probably the ratio of debt to equity. That is the ratio of long-term loans to shareholders' funds. This can be measured in terms of nominal value or market value. Another common approach is to calculate the percentage of debt to total capital (debt plus equity). See also the notes on borrowing ratio, equity gearing and income gearing.

Gross profit The difference between sales and the cost of goods sold.

Historic cost convention The convention by which assets are valued on the basis of the original cost of acquiring or producing them.

Income gearing This ratio highlights the profits available to meet the company's interest payments. It is defined as interest paid expressed as a percentage of pre-interest, pre-tax profit (EBIT). It is the reciprocal of interest cover.

Interest cover The relationship between the amount of profit (before interest and before tax) and the amount of interest payable during a period.

Liability   An amount owed.

Liquidity   A term used to describe the cash resources of a business and its ability to meet its short-term obligations.

Listed investments   Investments the market price for which is quoted on a recognized stock exchange. They may therefore be traded on that exchange.

Long-term liability   An amount payable more than 12 months after the balance sheet date.

Market price   The price of a quoted security for dealing in the open market.

Net assets   The amount of total assets less total liabilities.

Net book value   The cost (or valuation) of fixed assets less accumulated depreciation to date. Net book value bears no relationship to market value.

Net current assets   The amount of current assets less current liabilities.

Net realizable value   Amount at which an asset could be sold in its existing condition at the balance sheet date, after deducting any costs to be incurred in disposing of it.

Nominal value   The face value of a share or other security.

Overhead   Any expense, other than the direct cost of materials or labour involved in making a company's products.

Prepayment   The part of a cost which is carried forward as an asset in the balance sheet to be recognized as an expense in the ensuing period(s) in which the benefit will be derived from it, e.g. the payment in advance of rates.

Price/earnings ratio (P/E)   The relationship between the market price of a share and its latest reported earnings per share.

Profit   The difference between the revenues earned in the period and the costs incurred in earning them. A number of alternative definitions are possible according to whether the figure is struck before or after tax, distributions, etc.

Profit and loss A statement summarizing the revenues and the costs incurred in earning them during an accounting period.

Provision The amount written off in the current year's profit and loss account in respect of an obligation where the amount or timing is uncertain.

Quick ratio The ratio of those current assets readily convertible into cash (usually current assets less stock) to current liabilities.

Revaluation reserve The increase in value of a fixed asset as a result of a revaluation. This needs to be included in the balance sheet as part of shareholders' funds in order to make the balance sheet balance.

Revenue reserves The accumulated amount of profit less losses, generated by the company since its incorporation and retained in it. It may be called by other names.

Revenue Money received from selling the product of the business.

Share capital Stated in the balance sheet at its nominal value and (if fully paid, and not subject to any share premium) representing the amount of money introduced into the company by its shareholders at the time the shares were issued.

Shareholders' funds A measure of the shareholders' total interest in the company, represented by the total of share capital plus reserves.

Share premium The surplus over and above nominal value received in consideration for the issue of shares.

Turnover Revenue from sales.

Variable cost A cost that increases or decreases in line with changes in the level of activity.

Working capital Current assets less current liabilities, representing the amount a business needs to invest – and which is continually circulating – in order to finance its stock, debtors and work-in-progress.

Work-in-progress Goods (or services) in the course of production (or provision) at the balance sheet date.

Answers to the Smart Tests

1. True.

2. None, once the company has issued the shares and been paid for them, their market value does not in the short-term affect the financial position of the business. Shareholders who sell at that point have lost the money due to the lowering of the market, or second hand, value of their holding. It might, of course, come up again and restore the original value.

3. It goes down.

4. It goes down.

5. Each buying and selling transaction is counted so the number of shares traded is half the amount shown or 14.186 million.

6. Now that really is up to you.

7. £108,000 × 0.05% =£54 per day £54 × 40 =£2,160 £2,160 is 2% of £108,000.

8. The gross margin is 20% (25/125).

9   The gross margin is 37.5% (600/1,600).

10 The packaged holiday company.

11 By its capability to produce profits.

12 Price–earnings and yield.

13 Up, since the amount in shares issued goes down by the value of the number of the shares sold.

14 It goes up, at least in the short term.

15 It goes up. This is an instant way of improving this ratio.

16 Worse. Since they are inflating stock by a figure which will never go into sales revenue, they are making their stock turnover period look longer.

17 755. Simply add the two numbers and divide by 2 to get a reasonable approximation.

18 Number 2 is more likely to be the problem if the whole team is suffering. There seems to be a physical limit to how much of their time the average salesperson will spend with customers. There is rarely much scope there for improvement.

19 No they make less. They would be better to get the departments to pay their phone bills directly to the phone company.

20 Since depreciation has increased, your profit goes down and so does your return on assets performance. It has no impact on cashflow.

21 £337,500.

22 Many people do this but it does not make much sense. After all, you wanted them to sell more didn't you? If you think they are going to earn too much relative to other staff, then adjust the amount of the bonus rather than set a cap.

23 (a) The annual cashflow goes position in year 6 and the project breaks even in year 10.
(b) 149,302,000 since that is the largest number in the accumulated cashflow.
21,005,991 for the same reason.

24

Timing of cashflow	Amount of cashflow	Discount factor at 15%	Present value
Immediate	(20,000)	1.00	(20,000)
After 1 year	10,000	0.870	8,700
After 2 years	8,000	0.756	6,048
After 3 years	6,000	0.658	3,948
Net present value			(1,304)

Since the net present value is negative, the company should reject this project.

26 Approximately 7.6%. More precisely 7.4% allowing for the effect of inflation.

Index

accounting concepts 209
accounting policies 209
accounts payable 209
accrual 209
accruals concept 209
analysts 37–8
annual reports 78, 80, 83, 86
    smart test 218
assets 209
    current 100–2
    return on 97–8
auditors 40

balance sheet 210
    current assets
        cash 55
        debtors 55
        stock 55
    current liabilities
        creditors 57–8
        dividend 58
        overdraft 58
        short-term loans 58
        tax 58
    described 53–4
    example 60
    external liabilities

        long-term loans 58
        provisions for liabilities/charges 59
    fixed assets
        intangible 56
        tangible 55
    shareholders' funds
        minority interests 59
        reserves 65–6
        share capital 59
    smart test 56, 218
balanced scorecard 144–5
    customer service 145
    environment 145, 146
    profits 145
    quality 145, 146
bankers' acceptance facility 197
banks 16
bookkeeping/accountancy 31
borrowing ratio 210
British Aerospace (BAe) 43
budgets
    administration costs 153
    battle of 148
    capital expenditure 153
    described 147–50
    manufacturing 153

budgets – *continued*
  motivation 157–8
  objectives 150
  problems
    predicting demand 154–6
    predicting production costs 156
    slack 156–7
  production 153
  selling/distribution 153
  setting 150–4
  smart test 152, 219

capital employed 210
capital expenditure 45
capital expenditure/financial
    investment 63
  described 61–2
  equity dividends paid 64
  financing 64
  increase/decrease in cash in the
    period 64
  net cashflow from operating
    activities 62–3
  reconciliation of net cash flow to
    movement in net debt 65
  returns on investment/servicing
    of finance 63
  taxation 63
capital markets 203–4
  commercial paper 205
  debentures 204
  discounted bonds 204–5
cash 207
  use of 41
cashflow 173–5, 210
  discounted 179–88
  smart tests 177, 184, 219
cashflow statement, acquisitions/
    disposals 63–4
chairman's statements 78, 80, 83, 86

Companies Act 115
Compusell Inc. 98, 208
  asset turnover 106
  balance sheet 60
  budget setting 153, 155
  capital gearing 73
  depreciation 45
  described 12
  gross margins 50
  inception to seven years old 77–8
    annual report 78
    ratios 78
  7 to 15 years 79–80
    annual report 80
    investors' ratios 81–2
    ratios 80–1
  15 to 23 years 82–3
    annual report 83
    investors' ratios 84
    ratios 84
  over 25 years 85–6
    annual report 86
    investors' ratios 87–8
    ratios 87
  information dissemination 130
  investment appraisal 159–60,
    162–3, 168, 170–1
  investment in 17–18
  liquidity 103
  management accounts 116,
    136–8, 143
  P/E ratio in 31
  profit and loss account 131–2
  profit ratios 99
  raising capital 205
  rating 31
  return on capital employed 75
  shares dropped 25
  smart test 33, 217
  spreadsheets 92–3

Compusell Inc. – *continued*
  stock 105
  upgraded 38
  Wall Street Journal listing 31–2
consistency concept 210
contribution method 134–6
corporate finance
  defined 8
  flow chart 10
  jargon 7
  knowledge 2–3
  profitability 4
corporate ratios
  benchmarks 77–88
  capital gearing 71–3
  familiarity with financial
    information 89–90
  income gearing 73–4
  overview 67–71
  pre-tax profit margin 76
  return on capital employed 75
  smart test 75, 218
costs
  avoidance of future 167
  estimate 168–70
  reduction 165–7
  weigh up risks 170–2
costs of goods sold 210
costs of sales 210
creative accounting 47, 51, 56, 57,
    58, 61, 108, 109, 135
creditors 210
current asset 210
current cost 210
current liability 210
current ratio 211

debentures 211
debtors 211
decision making 159–61

deferred asset/liability 211
deferred taxation 211
depreciation 45, 211
directors 39
discounted cashflow 179–80
  comments on 183–8
  mechanics 180–2
  in practice 185–8
distribution 211
dividend cover 79, 211
dividend yield 211
dividends 52
Dow Jones 32

earnings per share (EPS) 51–2, 211
EBIT (earnings before interest and
    tax) 51
employees 110–14
  average wage per employee
    113–14
  profit per employee 1112–13
  sales per employee 111–12
equity gearing 211
exceptional item 211
expected value analysis 189–90
expense 212
extraordinary item 212

finance
  non-equity capital 196–203
  raising capital from capital
    markets 203–7
  smart test 195, 219
  sources 193–5
  use of computers 198
  what if? questions 198
financial statements
  balance sheet 53–61
  cashflow 61–5
  notes to the accounts 60

financial statements – *continued*
  profit and loss account 46–53
Financial Times
  Annual Reports service 90
  article information
    commodity news 35–6
    currency news 35
    economic news 35
    financial news 36
    industrial news 35
    marketing news 36
  column headings 22, 90
    ex-dividend (xd) 24–5
    industry sectors 22
    price movement 25
    price-earnings (P/E ratio) 3027–8
    sector averages 22
    volume '000s 26
    yield 26–7
  page information
    adverts 34–5
    front page 34
    sample of contents 33
    strategy news 36
    index 34
    listings 21
fixed asset 212
fixed cost 212

gearing 107–10, 212
  capital ratio 107–9
  income ratio 109–10
gearing ratios 212
general business model 41–6
gross profit 212
growth management 77

Hamel, Gary 94
HAR plc 208

asset turnover 106
balance sheet 57
budget setting 151–2, 154, 155–6, 157–8
buying 19–20
capital gearing 72–3
comparison of ratios 89
described 12–13
employee ratios 112–13
FT listing 23, 25–8
gearing 108
investment appraisal 162, 163, 164–5, 167
liquidity in 103
long-term strategy 199
management accounting 124–8, 136–8, 143
profit and loss account 52
profit margin 76
profit ratios 99
rating 30
recruitment 30
spreadsheets 92–3
stock 105
venture capital 201
high-low yields 25, 27
historic cost convention 212

IBM 49
ICL 61
income gearing 212
interest cover 213
Internet companies 206
inventory *see* stock
investment
  analysts 37–8
  basics 16
    buying shares 17–20
    depositing in a bank 16–17
    stock exchange listings 21

investment – *continued*
  Financial Times 21–31
  FT/Wall Street Journal page layouts 32–7
  Wall Street Journal 32
investment appraisal 159–60
  choose a timescale 162–4
  compare possible projects, risks, benchmarks
    discounted cashflow 179–88
    payback period 175–8
    return on capital employed 179
  estimate benefits 164
    avoidance of future costs 167
    improvement in control 168
    increase in revenue 164–5
    reduction in costs 165–7
  estimated costs 168–70
  expected value analysis 189–90
  optimistic/most likely/pessimistic estimates 190–1
  produce cashflow 173–5
  produce projected profit and loss account 172–3
  risk analysis 188–91
  weigh up risks to costs and benefits 170–2
investors 13–14

just in time (JIT) 44

legislation 39–40
leverage 202
liability 213
liquidity 213
listed investments 213
loan capital 194–5
London Stock Exchange 21
long-term liability 213

management accounts 115–17
  attributes
    clear information 129–30
    communication 123–4
    comparison and trends 130
    contribution method of allocating costs 134–6
    control 128–9
    credibility 126–7
    critical success factors 124–6
    reporting system 132–4
  converting profit and loss into cashflow 143–4
  operating leverage 141–3
  responsible 138–41
  smart test 116, 127, 219
  work to balanced score card 145–6
market price 213

net assets 213
net book value 213
net current assets 213
net present value (NPV) 183–4
net realizable value 213
nominal value 213
non-equity capital 196–7
  long-term 202–3
  medium term
    bank loans 199
    government grants 200
    leasing/hire purchase 199–200
    loan guarantee scheme 200
  short-term 197
  venture capital 200–2

operating leverage 141–3
overhead 213

Packard, David 95

payback method 193–7
planning see budgets
prepayment 213–14
price/earnings (P/E) ratio 18–19, 27–8, 29, 214
   smart tests 21, 28, 217
production
   budgets 153
   predicting costs 156
profit 95, 214
   margin 96–7
profit centre management 119–22
   smart test 123, 219
profit and loss account 214
   administrative overheads 50
   converting into cashflow 143–4
   described 46–8
   dividends 47–8
   example 52
   gross margin 49–50
   gross profit 48–9
   net profit before tax 52
   projected 172–3
   retained profit 52
   sales turnover 48
   selling/distribution expenses 50
   smart tests 49, 50, 218
   tax 52
   trading profit 51
provision 214

quick ratio 102–3, 214

ratios 67, 79, 80–1, 83, 87
   corporate 68–90
   derived from annual report 91–3
      asset utility 103–7
      current assets 100–2
      gearing 120–3
      growth 94–5

liquidity 99
profit margin 96–7
profitability 95
quick or acid test 102–3
return on assets 97–8
return on capital employed 95–6
return on shareholders' funds 98–9
   employee 110–14
   investors' 79, 81–2, 84, 87–8
   reliance on 70–1
   shareholder 13–38
   smart test 97, 218
return on capital employed (RoCE) 75, 84, 95–6, 179
   smart test 95, 218
revaluation reserve 214
revenue 214
revenue expenditure 44–5
revenue reserves 214
risk analysis 164, 170–2, 188–91

sensitivity analysis 188
share capital 193–4, 214
share premium 215
shareholders 13–16
   funds 215
   return on funds 98–9
shares
   buying/selling 17–20
   cost and risk 18
   dividends 17
   P/E ratio 18–19
   smart tests 22, 27, 33, 37, 217, 218
   trading 19
   value 15
Smart Autos 119–22
Smith, Terry 47

spreadsheets 197–8
stock, smart test 43, 219
stock turnover 103–5
strategy 117–18
suppliers 100, 101

tax 52, 185–6
term loans 197
Tesco 43
turnover 215

smart test 107, 219

variable cost 215
venture capital 200–2
venture capitalists 5–6, 80

Wall Street Journal 31–2
work-in-progress 215
working capital 215
    cycle 41–2